"If we want to thrive and flourish in life, we need to be able to interact and communicate effectively with one other. In *People Skills*, Debra shows us how. This book is practical, relatable, helpful, and needed in these times."

—**Christine Caine**, founder A21 and Propel Women

"In *People Skills*, Debra Fileta equips believers to build better relationships—not just through insight, but through humility, self-awareness, and biblical wisdom. This book offers practical steps for anyone wanting to love others like Jesus does."

—**Jonathan Pokluda**, lead pastor of Harris Creek Baptist Church, best-selling author, and host of the podcast *Becoming Something*

"It doesn't matter how talented, brilliant, or experienced you are if you lack emotional intelligence. Few things will set you up for success as much as strong people skills—or hold you back as much as the lack of them. From her vast experience helping people navigate their hangups as a counselor, Debra Fileta has written a modern take on the ever-important subject of winning friends and influencing people. *People Skills* will help you take ownership of the way you connect and communicate. This is a book you'll want to revisit again and again."

—**Levi Lusko**, author of *Blessed Are the Spiraling*

"In *People Skills*, Debra Fileta reminds us that one of the most empowering choices we can make is to take ownership of our relationships. With clarity, courage, and grace, she equips us with the tools to love well, communicate clearly, and cultivate connections that truly reflect God's design. This book is a must-read for anyone who wants to grow in wisdom and strength in every relationship."

—**Todd and Julie Mullins**, senior pastors, Christ Fellowship Church

"In our world today, we are letting technology prevent us from developing the skills we desperately need to interact with others in our lives. What a tragedy! The book you hold in your hands is a response to this modern-day phenomenon. We must learn people skills to be fully human and to understand how to live with true empathy, wisdom, and kindness—virtues that our technology will never be able to teach us."

—**Katherine Wolf**, author of *Treasures in the Dark*, *Suffer Strong*, and *Hope Heals*

PEOPLE SKILLS

DEBRA FILETA M.A., LPC

HARVEST HOUSE PUBLISHERS
EUGENE, OREGON

Cover design by Faceout Studio, Spencer Fuller

Cover images © gaga.vastard / Shutterstock

Interior design by KUHN Design Group

For bulk, special sales, or ministry purchases, please call 1-800-547-8979.
Email: CustomerService@hhpbooks.com

This logo is a federally registered trademark of the Hawkins Children's LLC. Harvest House Publishers, Inc., is the exclusive licensee of this trademark.

People Skills
Copyright © 2026 by Debra Fileta
Published by Harvest House Publishers
Eugene, Oregon 97408
www.harvesthousepublishers.com

ISBN 978-0-7369-9109-4 (pbk)
ISBN 978-0-7369-9110-0 (eBook)
ISBN 978-0-7369-9426-2 (eAudio)

Library of Congress Control Number: 2025936270

Printed in the United States of America

25 26 27 28 29 30 31 32 33 34 / BP / 10 9 8 7 6 5 4 3 2 1

To my Buddy, Eli.

We've been practicing our people skills on each other practically every single day of your life.

Through the joys and through the challenges, I consider it a high privilege and an honor to be your mom.

When you were born, God told me that He would use your voice to share His love with the world.

My prayer is that your people skills would take you farther than you ever imagined, and that you would always convey God's love no matter where you go.

I love you, Buddy!

P.S. What time's the party?

CONTENTS

1

PEOPLE SKILLS

Why You Need Them (Not Just the Person You're Thinking Of)

Something surprising happened while I was writing this book, which I think is very telling. In fact, it's something that's never happened during the writing process of any of my eight other books. Because writing is a consistent part of my life, it's not uncommon for people to ask me a question such as "What are you writing about these days?" In response I usually go into a quick summary of the book, what it's about, and why I'm writing on this particular topic. Depending on what the book is about, I typically get a myriad of different responses (if you know anything about my previous books, I'm sure you can guess which title gets the biggest reaction!).[1]

But of all the different reactions I've gotten over the years, the most surprising ones came when I talked about the topic of this book. Whenever I told someone I was writing a book about people skills, they would all start by saying how interesting, much-needed, and timely the topic was for our specific culture. That wasn't the surprising part though. I mean, truth be told, we live in a culture where technology has replaced so many of our one-on-one relationships. For most of us, the little device in our pocket has surpassed our need to interact with real-life people in real-life ways.

Where you used to have to stop someone to ask what time it was, now you can glance at your phone and see the time any second of any day.

Where you used to have to go into a restaurant and talk to a waiter to order your food, you can now get it delivered to your doorstep without having to talk to anyone.

Where you used to have to go to the library and talk to the librarian to get help finding the book you needed for a topic you were researching, you can now find unlimited information within seconds from the comfort of your own home.

Where you used to have to leave your house to go grocery shopping, head to the mall, or run to the pharmacy, you can now order everything online with a click of a button, and choose the option, "leave it at my door," so you don't even have to see a human being if you don't want to.

We've outsourced people for devices.

In fact, it's gotten so bad that one survey found that over 40 percent of adults say they go days without seeing anyone face-to-face.[2] You can't develop people skills when you're not interacting with people. Our devices have replaced our need for people skills, and to be honest, that only scratches the surface of why we struggle so much in our relationships. This is such a complex and layered conversation.

So no, I'm not surprised that people see a need for a book like this. I think we'd all agree that our culture is desperately lacking in people skills. But what *did* surprise me is what they would say after they affirmed the need for this book. Almost 98 percent of the people I shared with would add a comment like this: "Oh, I definitely know someone who could use this book." Whether it was a husband, a friend, a coworker, a neighbor, or even our culture at large, everyone was quick to think of someone they knew who could use a book about people skills. But it was rare for someone to have the insight, awareness, and foresight to say: "I could really use that book myself."

To be honest, I find that reaction rather concerning, and I'll tell you why in a moment. But first, let me affirm that those of you who are reading this book right now are incredibly ahead of the game because you have enough self-awareness to acknowledge that, when it comes to interpersonal relationships, social connections, and everyday interactions, there will always be room to grow, learn, and transform. One of the most important parts of our lives is our social connections, and our people skills or lack thereof can literally make or break our relationships, which in turn can make or break our entire lives.

Not only do I believe that all of us need to take ownership of our people skills, but I'm also concerned with the common others-focused reaction. It's a reflection that, oftentimes, the people who need people skills the most aren't skilled enough to recognize their own deficit. We tend to want to look at the deficits of others long before looking at our own.

I AM THE RUDE ONE, THE INGRATE, THE THIEF

There's a story I read years ago called *The Cookie Thief* about a woman who was killing time at the airport, waiting for her flight. She went and bought herself a bag of cookies, and then sat down on a bench to read her book while she waited. Within a few moments, a gentleman came by and sat next to her. She tried to ignore him and kept her nose in her book, until the man reached his hand into her bag of cookies and started munching on them! The story, creatively written in poetic form, goes on to describe her shock and fury as she watched the man diminish her stash of cookies one, by one, by one: "She thought to herself as the minutes ticked by, 'If I wasn't so nice,

I would blacken his eye.' With each cookie she took, he took one too, when only one was left, she wondered what he would do. With a smile on his face, and a nervous laugh, he took the last cookie and broke it in half. He offered her half, as he ate the other, she snatched it from him and thought…oooh, brother. This guy has some nerve and he's also rude, why he didn't even show any gratitude!" The story continues as the woman abruptly gathers her belongings and heads to her gate. She sits down in her seat on the plane and reaches into her bag to find…her very own unopened bag of cookies. "If mine are here, she moaned in despair, the others were his, and he tried to share. Too late to apologize, she realized with grief, that she was the rude one, the ingrate, the thief."

Talk about a moment of humility. She just got told, as the young people say. She had spent so much time focusing on the man's deficits, she completely missed her own. Human beings tend to see the flaws around them before they see the flaws within them. And I can't say it's surprising. In fact, I often see this tendency in my work as a counselor, especially when dealing with interpersonal issues in counseling. It's so much easier to see the shortcomings of others than it is to recognize our own.

Whether it's a couple's therapy session, or we're dealing with a family conflict issue, a friendship situation, or some other problem at work, church, or elsewhere, it's common for the person presenting the problem to start their story by painting me a detailed picture of everyone else's deficits: "Here's what everyone else is doing wrong." I listen patiently (at least for a little while), but I've been a counselor long enough to know that the first story is never the full story. Eventually, in order to make any progress in any situation, there has to be a level of ownership. For true change and healing to happen, the story eventually has to turn from the narrative of what *they* are doing wrong to the narrative of what *you* can do differently. Because we can't really see the story clearly until we start with ourselves.

FOR TRUE CHANGE AND HEALING TO HAPPEN, THE STORY EVENTUALLY HAS TO TURN FROM THE NARRATIVE OF WHAT *THEY* ARE DOING WRONG TO THE NARRATIVE OF WHAT *YOU* CAN DO DIFFERENTLY.

This isn't merely a good counseling strategy. The Bible affirms this approach in Matthew 7 saying,

> Why do you look at the speck of sawdust in your brother's eye and pay no attention to the plank in your own eye? How can you say to your brother, "Let me take the speck out of your eye," when all the time there is a plank in your own eye? You hypocrite, first take the plank out of your own eye, and then you will see clearly to remove the speck from your brother's eye (verses 3-5).

The healthiest people lead the way in ownership by always asking, *What's my role?* Because if you have no role, you also have no control. If you have no role, you can't change the outcome. Having a role means having influence and the ability to change your situation because you can choose to do things differently. And this is especially true when it comes to your interpersonal relationships.

HOW TO CHANGE THE RECIPE

If you're ever in a counseling session with me, at some point you will likely hear me explain that relationships are kind of like a recipe. You hold a portion of the ingredients, and the people around you hold a portion of the ingredients too. You can't change someone else's ingredients, but you *can* change your own, and that change is enough to influence the outcome of the entire recipe! When it comes to relationships and interacting with people, we have to be acutely aware that we can't force the people around us to change, heal, adjust, mature, or grow. While we can't change the people around us, we can change what we bring to the recipe of the relationship. We can change ourselves. We can set better boundaries, learn to communicate more effectively, take inventory of our body language, respond instead of react, overcome our insecurities, deal with our personal triggers, and use so many other relationship-changing skills we'll learn throughout the pages of this book. You can't change someone else, but you can change yourself, which can influence the entire relationship.

YOU CAN'T CHANGE SOMEONE ELSE'S INGREDIENTS, BUT YOU *CAN* CHANGE YOUR OWN, AND THAT CHANGE IS ENOUGH TO INFLUENCE THE OUTCOME OF THE ENTIRE RECIPE!

I have a feeling you are the type of person who believes this to be true, because here you are reading this book. And the fact that you are here gives me hope. It tells me that you are insightful enough to believe that maybe there's something you can learn, change, or adjust in how you come across to others, how you relate to people, as well as how you interact in relationships. It assures me that you know the only way to make significant changes in our world, our community, our churches, and our families is by taking ownership of our own changes. Because we know that instead of blaming culture, we have to influence culture. And so instead of just giving this book to that person you thought of, you're reading it for yourself. And for that, I can confidently say: You're my kind of people.

With that said, let me give you some insider information. The most difficult thing about the topic of people skills is that, just like any skill set, there's a learning curve to getting them right. It takes practice, trial-and-error, insight, self-awareness, and a commitment to doing relationships well. So get yourself ready, grab a friend to join you if you'd like (or maybe that person you were thinking of in the beginning of this book), and let's spend some time looking at the skills we bring to the table, taking ownership of how we come across in our interactions, and committing to doing relationships to the best of our ability. It's time to take ownership of our people skills. Because your relationships are only as strong as your skills.

TAKE OWNERSHIP

1. When it comes to the topic of people skills, was there someone who came to mind (other than yourself) who could use this topic? How can you shift your perspective to focus on your personal growth in this area?

2. Do you tend to take ownership and acknowledge your personal role in any interpersonal conflict, misunderstanding, or dilemma, or do you have a tendency to deflect ownership and responsibility?

3. What is one area in which you have seen a deficit in your people skills, and how has it affected your personal life and relationships? (For example: difficulty handling conflict, struggles expressing emotions, poor listening skills, a lack of communication skills, difficulty taking ownership and apologizing, or struggling with shyness or insecurity.)

4. "We've outsourced people for devices" (page 10). Reflect on this statement and whether or not it's true in your life. If

true, consider how you can set yourself up to begin practicing your people skills by being intentional about increasing your interactions with real-life people over the course of reading this book.

2

IT'S NOT A DEFICIT OF LOVE

It's a Deficit of Skill

It's not a deficit of love," I said to them in the middle of our couple's session. "It's a deficit of skill." In theory, Theo loved his wife Lisa more than anything in this world, which is why he just couldn't comprehend how Lisa was doubting his love for her. Sometimes, he felt as though they were speaking different languages, and he couldn't seem to get past the language barrier. When they came to see me for marriage counseling, I quickly sensed that this had very little to do with a lack of love and much more to do with a lack of skill. Theo really did love his wife, but he had never learned how to communicate that love on a practical or emotional level. He often came across as distracted, apathetic, and uninterested in her, though that was the exact opposite of what he felt toward her. He had never learned how to ask curious questions, or taken inventory of his body language, eye contact, and facial expressions. He'd also never learned how to practice active listening while she was talking, speak with a tender tone, or even how to communicate back to her in a way that was meaningful to her.

His efforts weren't getting through to her because he lacked the skill set and didn't know the action steps to convey his love in a way that made sense to Lisa. Their marriage struggles weren't due to a lack of love; they were due to a lack of skill. A skill set that Theo, along with so many other men and women whom I have encountered, had never been taught. And maybe as you read this book, you'll find yourself in that category too, whether or not you realize it right at this moment.

HIGH IN LOVE, LOW IN SKILL

In my work as a licensed professional counselor, I've interacted with so many people just like Theo, who are high in love and good intentions, but really low in their people skills. Their lack of skills inhibits their ability to communicate the love that's in their heart, and so much of how we convey love is in the practical, day-to-day things. They may come across as unloving or uncaring, apathetic or aloof, cool and distant, distracted or uninterested, but really, they're just lacking in their ability to express their emotions, take inventory of their body language, convey empathy, or be intentional with their tone. I often find myself using the phrase, "It's not a deficit of love; it's a deficit of skill." There is a certain skill set that you need to learn to be able to thoroughly and effectively communicate what's in your heart to the people around you and make sure you're coming across the way you intend. And it's a skill set that I believe has the power to make or break your relationships. Because your relationships can only be as strong as your skills.

I find it so fascinating that when we read the "love" chapter in Scripture, the one that's read at almost every wedding we've ever been to, the tangible concept of love is described, not as a feeling, but as a list of practical actions. There's a skill set to learning how to love well. This well-known passage says,

> Love is patient, love is kind. It does not envy, it does not boast, it is not proud. It does not dishonor others, it is not self-seeking, it is not easily angered, it keeps no record of wrongs. Love does not delight in evil but rejoices with the truth. It always protects, always trusts, always hopes, always perseveres. Love never fails (1 Corinthians 13:4-8).

DC Talk said it best when they coined their 1992 hit song, "Luv Is a Verb." Love isn't conveyed simply by how you feel toward someone; it's conveyed through a series of actions. It's about what you choose to do and choose not to do.

This is why looking at your own people skills is crucial. Not only is it crucial to the health of your closest relationships, it's also an influential part of the impact you will have in this world. Your people skills matter more than you realize, because they set the stage for how you come across to others as well as your effectiveness in the way you show love. Your people skills pave the way for the intentions of your heart to get communicated in a way that's meaningful and impactful to the people around you. Your people skills will either convey your love or convolute your love.

YOUR PEOPLE SKILLS WILL EITHER CONVEY YOUR LOVE OR CONVOLUTE YOUR LOVE.

As people of God, we are called to love. In fact, love is not only the evidence of who we are (Christians), but it is also the evidence of *whose* we are (God's children). John 13:34-35 reminds us that this is how we will be recognized and set apart: "A new command I give you: Love one another. As I have loved you, so you must love one another. By this everyone will know that you are my disciples, if you love one another." Loving others is crucial, but learning how to convey that love is just as crucial.

Think about a time in your life when a meaningful relationship was strained (whether your marriage, family member, friend, acquaintance, or coworker) due to a misunderstanding, difference in perspectives, an inability to work through a conflict, unaddressed hurts, a lack of intentionality, or something else. There's a good chance the tension could have either been resolved or alleviated with a healthy dose of people skills. In fact, I think the definition of people skills could be wrapped up like this: *A practical understanding of how we allow the love that God has given us to be conveyed to the people closest to us.* It's the skill set we need in order to communicate the love that we've been given. But if that's actually the case, then we need to take seriously the fact that a *lack* of those same skills can then inhibit the way we show love too.

PEOPLE SKILLS ARE A PRACTICAL UNDERSTANDING OF HOW WE ALLOW THE LOVE THAT GOD HAS GIVEN US TO BE CONVEYED TO THE PEOPLE CLOSEST TO US.

WHAT COULD A LITTLE MORE SKILL DO?

My husband came home from work recently and shared an insightful story about an older gentleman who had come into his eye clinic that day (for those of you who don't know, my husband is an ophthalmologist) and wreaked havoc on just about everyone he encountered. This gentleman was disgruntled, grumpy, belligerent, and straight up degrading to all of the staff he interacted with. The office staff was so offended and thrown off by his over-the-top rude behavior that they requested he be removed as a patient because they couldn't handle dealing with him again. So John set up a meeting to talk with the disgruntled gentleman.

John worked hard to respond to him with a compassionate and curious tone, even when met with his negativity and grumpiness. He asked sincere questions and tried to really listen to the gentleman. He allowed the love in his heart to be conveyed through his tone, his body language, his thoughtful questions, his listening stance, and his gentle responses. Eventually, the gentleman shared that he had recently lost his wife and was dealing with the deep void her absence had left. In addition to this, literally the day before his eye appointment, he received a detrimental cancer diagnosis, and was now left to deal with this hard news all by himself. He got emotional as he apologized for his behavior, and when the rest of the staff understood what was going on in his life, they were able to respond to him with compassion rather than contempt.

In my opinion, this is a clear example of how a healthy dose of people skills paved a way for a difficult situation to be alleviated rather than aggravated. Even in a difficult situation, John was able to convey what was in his heart toward the gentleman (love, care, and concern) through practical ways (listening skills, curious questions, empathy, body language, and tone). His skill set in that situation doesn't dismiss or excuse the gentleman's behavior, but it's a skill set that certainly contributed to a positive outcome. Your people skills have so much influence and the power to convey or to convolute what's actually going on in your heart.

Throughout the chapters of this book we're going to dive deep into exactly what it looks like to practice this important skill set, whether in the context of a difficult social situation or in the context of everyday interactions; whether in your closest relationships or with the people you come across each day; whether you're interacting with someone who is hurt, angry, or offended or whether you're simply trying to express your affection to someone you deeply care for.

We're going to take inventory of our ability to convey love or our tendency to convolute it through skills such as our ability to listen actively, have appropriate body language and facial expressions, adjust our tone and tenderness, ask curious questions, practice empathy and understanding, offer proper apologies, gauge our personality temperature, assess our ability to give and receive feedback, deal with difficult people and situations, and so much more. But for now, I want you to sit with this question and answer honestly: Are my people skills serving me by conveying my love, or sabotaging me by convoluting my love? What could a little more skill do for you?

TAKE OWNERSHIP

1. Think of a relational strain or conflict that came up in your life recently. If you had to narrow down one to two words to describe the reason for the conflict, what would they be? ______________________________ (Examples: misunderstanding, hurt feelings, different perspectives, etc.)

   How could having more people skills have impacted this situation?

2. List some ways that your people skills have *conveyed* your love to the people around you.

3. List some ways that your people skills (or lack thereof) have *convoluted* your love.

4. If someone close to you were to assess your people skills, what is one thing they would list as your strength? ______________________ What is one thing they would list as your weakness? ______________________ If you're brave (and I know you are), invite someone close to you to answer this question for you and compare what you wrote to what they said.

3

FIRST IMPRESSIONS

How Do You Come Across?

Imagine this: You're part of a social experiment. You're asked to walk into a room and then given no additional instructions. You open a door and step inside to see a room filled with 99 complete strangers and a few cameras mounted on all the walls. You find a spot to stand and start looking around at all the other unfamiliar faces who are also looking back at you. No one knows the purpose of the experiment, but everyone is aware that they are part of one. Some people are smiling, exuding warmth and lightness. Others look nervous, biting their nails or trying not to make eye contact. Some are loud and energetic, occupying the space in the room with their energy and charisma. Others are quiet and shy, trying not to be noticed. Slowly, smaller groups start to form out of the 100 strangers as people begin creating their social circles and making small talk with one another.

Here's my question to you regarding this situation: What's the first impression people will have of you? In other words, how would you come across in a social setting like that? Would it take you a little while to warm up to others, or would you be ready to interact as soon as you stepped in the room? Would you be the type of person to stand quietly against the wall, hoping no one will notice you, or would you be the one making new friends and telling stories within the first five minutes? Would your facial expressions and body language be warm and inviting, or would you come across as guarded and skeptical? Flip to the end of this chapter, and in the Take Ownership portion, take some time to put into words how you think you would come across in a social setting like this. If you're not totally sure, ask someone close to you to give you their perspective based on what they know of you.

Now that you've put into words how you think you come across in a social situation like this one, I want you to ask yourself this question: Why? Why do you come across the way that you do? The simple answer is, *That's just my personality*. But the more accurate yet complex answer is that underneath the surface of our lives, our social skills are fueled by a set of underlying beliefs and thoughts that influence how we behave. In my book *Reset*, I talk about the important formula that *Thoughts* lead to *Feelings* which lead to *Behaviors*.[1]

For example, if you walk into a room thinking, *I hope no one notices me because I am looking really rough today*, you're going to feel inadequate and insecure, which will then translate into behaviors that cause you to avoid standing out and being noticed. You might stand next to a wall to try to blend in, or make very little conversation. You might look down at the floor to try to avoid eye contact, or listen much more than you converse. To the rest of the group, you might come across as shy and quiet, which is just behavior that's being fueled by your negative thoughts underneath the surface.

In extreme contrast, if you walk into that same room believing, *I am a gift to these people and they are lucky to get to meet me today*, you're likely going to feel confident and even competitive. The behaviors that will flow out of those feelings could be talking too much paired with poor listening skills and lots of bragging. You might come across to others as self-centered and arrogant. But what's really having the greatest impact on how you come across are the underlying thoughts and beliefs you carry with you as you enter that room.

This is why taking ownership of our social skills, and particularly how we come across, requires a level of depth and intentionality. It's not just about learning a set of new behaviors; it's also about consistently being in tune to our default behaviors, as well as to what's underneath the surface driving those behaviors.

IT'S NOT JUST ABOUT LEARNING A SET OF NEW BEHAVIORS; IT'S ALSO ABOUT CONSISTENTLY BEING IN TUNE TO OUR DEFAULT BEHAVIORS, AS WELL AS TO WHAT'S UNDERNEATH THE SURFACE DRIVING THOSE BEHAVIORS.

HAS ANYONE EVER TOLD YOU?

"Has anyone ever told you that you come across cold and distant?" It was a pretty honest question I asked to a woman I had been working with in individual counseling for quite a while. She was wanting to work on her marriage, and part of that process meant we would also meet individually to work on the different dynamics each spouse contributed to the relationship. But as our sessions went on, it was hard for me to ignore the fact that her facial expressions were stone-cold and her demeanor was standoffish every time we met together, whether individually or as a couple. Her facial expressions were flat and very hard to read. She hardly smiled and looked as though she was constantly irritated (whether or not she was).

"No," she eventually replied to my direct question. "No one has told me that." (To be honest, I was kind of surprised that no one had ever mentioned her aloof demeanor, or that she slightly resembled the cousin of Jadis the White Witch from Narnia—but I'm not *that* direct.)

"Have you ever asked anyone to give you feedback on how you come across?" I responded.

"No," she said again. "I guess I never have."

That explains a lot, I thought.

Part of the problem is that we have such a biased perspective of how we come across. We're seeing our demeanor from the inside out, weighing our motives and our good intentions into the equation. But if we're the only ones we're consulting, we're not really getting an accurate view, are we? In fact, if you think about it, unless you're constantly in front of a mirror or viewing video footage of the replay of your social engagements, you never actually get to objectively *see* or *feel* how you come across to others. And even if we did have the impossible luxury of watching the play-by-play, we'd probably still watch the footage with our own biased internal narrations and interpretations. Our limited perspective comes down to the story we tell ourselves in our heads of how we *meant* to come across or *hoped* to come across, rather than how we actually came across.

OUR LIMITED PERSPECTIVE COMES DOWN TO THE STORY WE TELL OURSELVES IN OUR HEADS OF HOW WE *MEANT* TO COME ACROSS OR *HOPED* TO COME ACROSS, RATHER THAN HOW WE ACTUALLY CAME ACROSS.

Thankfully, I had a strong enough relationship with my client that she was able to trust me and really take into consideration my feedback about how she came across. I asked her what might be underneath the surface of her cool demeanor, and she paused for a while before responding, "You know...I think I have been hurt so many times over the years, that I've just built up these emotional walls around myself without even realizing it. I think my cold and detached demeanor is how I keep people from getting too close. Probably even my husband." The *why* underneath the surface of her demeanor was the belief that *I will get hurt if they get too close*, which fueled the way she came across to others, exuding an impression that kept people at a distance.

Have you ever invited someone you trust to give you feedback or a bit of constructive criticism with regard to the impression you give in social situations, whether in a group with 99 others or simply one-on-one? Has anyone ever told you their honest and direct perspective on both your social strengths and social weaknesses? If not, there's no better time to get some external data as you're taking ownership of how you come across to others. Allowing others to love us well, especially those we love and trust, means giving them permission: an invitation to speak into our lives with the truth in love (Ephesians 4:15).

Your first impressions matter, as well as the impressions that continue long after that. But what paves the way for that is your ability to understand *how* you come across, and most importantly *why* you come across that way.

TAKE OWNERSHIP

1. What are some words or phrases that describe how you might come across in the social experiment mentioned at the beginning of the chapter? If you need some help, feel free to borrow from the following list of words as a starting point: guarded, enthusiastic, charismatic, social, warm, inviting, friendly, shy, nervous, confident, loud, quiet, funny, insecure, uncomfortable, talkative, awkward, comfortable, skeptical, cautious, kind.

2. List some of the underlying thoughts you have about yourself or others as you enter a social situation. How do those thoughts influence how you feel in a social situation? How do those feelings influence how you behave in a social situation?

3. Have you ever invited someone to offer their feedback or constructive criticism regarding how you come across in social situations? If yes, write some of the responses others have given as your strengths as well as your weaknesses.

4. If you've never invited constructive criticism regarding how you come across in social interactions, who is someone you trust whom you could ask for feedback? Are you willing to ask them to point out your strengths as well as some of the things you could improve upon?

4

CONVERSATION SKILLS

Go Deeper with People

Have you ever interacted with someone with whom striking up a conversation felt like pulling teeth? I have. It was on my podcast to be exact. I have a hotline style show called *Talk To Me*, where people call in to the hotline and we have an on-air conversation that mimics a counseling session about whatever topic or issue they want to discuss. But in the early days of the podcast, I didn't have much of a filter of who joined me on the show. If you wanted to talk, you were invited to come and talk, which explains how I found myself in a 30 minute on-air conversation with a woman who actually didn't talk much! The irony of coming on a show called *Talk To Me,* but expecting *me* to do all the talking doesn't escape me. If that was the purpose of the show, I would have called it *Listen To Me Talk.* If a basic conversation requires a 50-50 commitment (you talk 50 percent and listen 50 percent), this conversation was more like a 95-5, with me doing most of the talking. And I found out very quickly it's really hard to have an on-air counseling session with yourself!

I'm not sure if the sweet girl had a case of stage fright that day, or if she was just a generally less-verbal person, but what I do know is that I had to work hard to fill what otherwise would have been what we call *dead air space*. Ironically, it ended up being a highly downloaded episode. I wonder if it's because her conversation skills (or more accurately, lack thereof) made everyone else feel better about their own deficits. Or maybe people just like listening to painstakingly awkward conversations. Who knows. Maybe I should experiment by increasing my awkward conversations ratio on the show just to see if my downloads increase this year.

Whether you are on the air or off the air, conversation skills are a legitimately important skill to have when it comes to interacting with people. In fact, many people would say it's on the top ten list of the most crucial people skills in both personal and professional relationships. Communication is the lifeline of a relationship, and being able to hold a conversation with back-and-forth dialogue is what initially cultivates a relationship and then keeps it alive. I often say to my clients that relationships are like a plant: give a relationship too much water, and it will die. But give it too little water, and it will also die. I think we can apply that principle to conversation as well. If you give too much (talk too much), the conversation will die. But if you give too little (talk too little), the conversation will also die. You don't want to drown a conversation with your own words, but you also don't want the conversation to dry out because of your lack of words.

Words convey interest. They invite people to go deeper. Earlier I talked about how our people skills can either convey or convolute our love, and our conversation skills have the power to do just that. You don't want to overpower a conversation with your thoughts, opinions, and ideas, but you also don't want to withhold so much that you seem uninterested and allow the conversation to stall. So here are a few things to consider as you're assessing and practicing your own conversation skills and your ability to go deeper with the people you interact with.

1. ASK OPEN-ENDED QUESTIONS

You may not know this, but one of the first things you learn in counseling graduate school is the art of asking open-ended questions to keep a conversation going. Without giving it much thought, we have a tendency of asking closed-ended questions, which lead the way to one-word answers, rather than paving the way for deeper conversations. For example, a closed-ended question would be: How was your day? To which the other person could respond with one word such as: Good! The alternate open-ended question would be something like: What was the best part of your day today? You can't answer that question with a one-word answer, which is why it's called an open-ended question. It paves the way for more conversation.

It's interesting how many people I hear from who are frustrated with their spouses, children, or friends for answering in one-word answers, all while they're unknowingly asking closed-ended questions. If you want more from someone in conversation, you've got to learn how to pave the way for more by asking good questions. This past Thanksgiving, my cousin came up to me to let me know what great conversationalists my children are becoming. Specifically, he told me how during dinner my son Eli turned to him and asked, "So, what are you enjoying about married life?" Which, he admitted, kind of threw him off coming from a 12-year-old boy! But he was pleasantly surprised at the invitation for deeper conversation. I was happy to hear that my kids are learning how to ask good questions, even if it does make for more talking than eating during Thanksgiving dinner.

As I've been immersed in the gospels lately, one thing I've noticed about Jesus is how often He asked questions. He asked so many open-ended questions that showed interest, care and concern, and conveyed that He wasn't after the quick answer. He wanted to go deeper with people, and His questions were always the invitation for more. According to biblical scholars, Jesus asked 307 questions throughout Scripture and only directly answered three questions.[1] Even as a little boy, He was intentional in asking questions (Luke 2:49). It makes me really consider my own tendency to ask questions in conversations, as well as my tendency to "have the answers." Am I truly wanting to go deeper with people, or am I more interested in giving my own opinions, thoughts, and ideas? Jesus modeled the importance of asking questions and inviting people to go deeper with Him.

JESUS MODELED THE IMPORTANCE OF ASKING QUESTIONS AND INVITING PEOPLE TO GO DEEPER WITH HIM.

Here are some more examples of open-ended questions you can use to make conversation:

- What was the hardest part of your day today?
- What is something you are looking forward to and why?
- What do you like about your career?
- What was the best part of your weekend?
- What are you enjoying about ______________?
- What has been the most difficult thing about __________?
- What do you think? What do you want? Why do you feel _______? (These are questions that Jesus Himself asked of others.)

Start to see open-ended questions as an essential part of your conversations and take initiative in using them to go deeper with people.

2. CONVEY GENUINE INTEREST

The most important part of having a good conversation probably comes down to genuine interest: do you actually care? Not, are you trying to get something out of this conversation, or to simply get through this conversation, but are you genuinely interested in this person and what this person has to say? No one is rating you on your ability to have a good conversation, because it's not about you to begin with. It's about your ability to convey love, care, concern, compassion, and kindness to the person you're interacting with. Whether it's a serious or superficial conversation makes no difference.

Often when people feel misunderstood, it's because there's been a lack of genuine interest displayed in the conversation. They wonder if you've really *seen* them. Another thing I admire about the conversation skills of Jesus is the genuine care and concern He had for the people He interacted with. He stopped what He was doing, allowed for interruptions, looked them in the eye, and got down on their level. He *saw* people (Matthew 9:20-22). What if we could see our conversations as an avenue to really *see* people? To really care about them? What if conversations weren't about what we "got out of them," but about our ability to convey God's love for the people we're conversing with? That mental shift alone would increase our conversation skills tenfold no matter who it is we're talking with.

3. LISTEN ACTIVELY

Being a good conversationalist means learning to really listen. Active listening is such an important skill that I'm going to spend an entire chapter on it later. It's so easy to let your mind wander during conversation, to get distracted by what's happening around you or what you are going to say next instead of really tuning in to what the person in front of you is saying. For me, the most embarrassing moments are when I forget someone's name after they literally just told it to me three seconds ago. And it's not because I didn't hear it; it's because I didn't really listen and receive it. My mind was distracted, and I wasn't really there. Listening requires you to be present in the moment and actively receive what's being conveyed to you with genuine interest. This requires us to clear our minds and shift our mindset in order to have a meaningful conversation.

4. SHARE YOUR PERSPECTIVE

Having a good conversation invites you to give as well as receive. If you ask too many questions without being intentional about sharing something in return, the conversation starts to feel like a job interview or an interrogation rather than a relational investment. Back to the analogy of the plant, you don't want to drown the conversation with your perspective, but you also don't want to withhold it. You want to walk away feeling like you learned something about them, and they learned something about you. I know people who are great at asking questions, but not so good at sharing about themselves in return. In fact, drilling someone with questions can actually be used as a deflection mechanism: a way to keep a conversation going without having to be vulnerable or share anything personal. It's intentionally keeping the spotlight on someone else to avoid having it on you, so that you don't have to give emotionally or relationally. That might work to get you through a given interaction, but it certainly doesn't strengthen relationships or build emotional equity. So take inventory of your ability to receive *and* to give in a conversation.

HAVING A GOOD CONVERSATION INVITES YOU TO GIVE AS WELL AS RECEIVE.

I genuinely believe that good conversation can usher us into spiritually significant interactions, and Scripture affirms this: "Let your conversation be always full of grace, seasoned with salt, so that you may know how to answer everyone" (Colossians 4:6). Just like salt is the substance that adds flavor to the ingredients, your conversation skills can add flavor to an interaction and take it from superficial to supernatural. You get to choose if your conversation skills will convey love or convolute it.

TAKE OWNERSHIP

1. On a scale of talking too much (ten) to talking too little (zero) in a conversation, what number would you rate yourself?

2. Which of the four conversation skills listed in this chapter do you need to work on strengthening? What can you do differently moving forward?

3. List three open-ended questions you will use in conversation this coming week. What is a mindset shift you can make to help you see conversations as an invitation to go deeper with people?

4. Do you have a harder time listening during a conversation (receiving), or sharing about yourself (giving)? Why does this tend to be hard for you? What is something you can do to challenge yourself in this specific area?

5

HOW DEEP ARE YOU?

Four Levels of Communication

If an emotionally deep conversation were like an ocean, my husband says I'm like a scuba diver that could wade in the deep end for hours on end without ever coming up for air. He says (with a smirk) that he, on the other hand, is more of a duck floaty kind of guy, content to bob around above the surface of the water in the shallow end for as long as possible. But with nearly 20 years of marriage under our belt, we've learned the importance of the different levels of depth when it comes to emotional connection and communication in our relationship. You can't live in your duck floaty forever, and you also have to learn to come up for air.

If you were to spend some time with me in my counseling office, one of the lessons we'd certainly cover in our time together would be about the four levels of communication. What surprises me the most about this topic is how few people grasp that there are different levels to the way we communicate. Many people were brought up in a family of origin where conversation wasn't very deep. Conversations stayed basic and superficial. So naturally, it's hard to recognize the different levels of depth if you've never been exposed to them.

But there is a different level of depth, intimacy, and connection based on the content that's being discussed. The deeper you go conversationally, the more intimate your relationship gets. The more vulnerable you are, the more significant your connection becomes. So whether you're a duck floaty kind of person, or a scuba diver like me, let's take a dive into the four different levels, because each one has a role and a purpose.

THE MORE VULNERABLE YOU ARE, THE MORE SIGNIFICANT YOUR CONNECTION BECOMES.

LEVEL 1 CONVERSATION: FACTS

The first level of conversation is the most basic, because it's the kind of conversation you can have with a stranger. It goes into the basic facts of life, answering questions of who, what, where, when, and why. You'll likely start with this type of conversation when you're meeting someone for the first time and making small talk. It's the type of conversation that asks questions like: *What do you do for a living? What's the weather like this weekend? What are your plans today? How long have you been working for this company? How many children do you have? When did you move to this area?*

Facts-based conversations don't require vulnerability because they are sharing the basics of life. It's the most superficial level of interacting with someone, yet it's important to start here when you're getting to know someone. Not only that, but this level of conversation is necessary for the day-to-day communication of life with your friends, family, and loved ones: *What's your schedule today? What time will you be home? Can you pick up milk after work? What are we having for dinner? Who is picking up the kids?* You can't get through life without basic facts, but the problem is too many people get comfortable with facts, because they don't require much relational depth. And as important as it is to have level 1 conversations as a part of your everyday life, you can't stay here and expect relational equity to develop.

LEVEL 2 CONVERSATION: IDEAS AND OPINIONS

The next level of conversation goes a little deeper because it allows you to offer a little more of yourself. Instead of answering questions with the basic facts, it invites you to share your perspective and opinions on those facts. You're revealing more of yourself as you share your ideas and opinions with the people around you and as you ask for theirs. Now we're moving past facts such as *What time is your meeting today?* to discovering deeper opinions by asking *How do you think the meeting went?* We're moving past the basics of *What teams are playing today?* to the invitation into personal disclosure of *Which is your favorite team?* There's a little more self-disclosure in level 2 conversations that help a person get to know you and you to get to know them. *What did you think of dinner? Where would you rather go on vacation? How did you like the movie? Which is your favorite book?* This level of conversation requires you to offer up a little more of yourself, but it also invites a deeper connection with the person you're communicating with.

LEVEL 3 CONVERSATION: FEELINGS

Now we've reached my comfort zone level. Get ready for the scuba gear, because level 3 conversation takes it a little deeper. But it's also the level of conversation where many people get stuck or confused. The ability to understand your feelings and then share them is a skill that the average person has to intentionally learn. Many people think they're sharing feelings, but they're actually sharing opinions. They believe they're engaging in a level 3 conversation, while they're still in level 2. I see this all the time in my counseling office with my clients. I might ask someone, "What did you feel when she said that to you?" And the response might be, "I felt like she didn't care!" That's not actually a feeling, though, is it? The idea that "she didn't care" is an opinion, not a feeling. Another example might be when someone asks you, "How are you feeling?" and you respond by saying, "I'm good." Good is not actually a feeling; it's a description of how things are. People tend to use descriptive words, rather than feeling vocabulary, and often they don't realize they're doing it. Just because you put the words "I feel" before an opinion or description doesn't make it a feeling!

You may have a category of what you believe are "good feelings," such as happy, excited, joyful, ecstatic, hopeful, and confident. And you might have a category of what you believe are "bad feelings," such as sad, depressed, anxious, overwhelmed, and frustrated. But simply responding with "I'm good" or "I'm not doing good" isn't really getting into your feelings. Most counselors will tell you there's actually no such thing as "bad" feelings. Even though they might feel uncomfortable, all feelings are just a signal. It's how you respond that ushers you into healthy or unhealthy territory. But that's a lesson for another day. I couldn't help squeezing in this mini lesson while we were on the subject. I told you I love the deep end.

Feelings conversations are so important because they invite others into the depth of who you are and what you're experiencing. They require deeper vulnerability because it's a higher level of self-disclosure. We all have feelings, but whether we're willing to acknowledge and then express them is what makes the difference in our connections. And like I said, this takes practice and intentionality. When you come from a family of origin where feelings weren't expressed, or worse yet, they were ignored, stuffed, or covered up, you start to believe that expressing how you feel is a sign of weakness. This is why it takes intentionality to change your beliefs and understand that feelings are actually the very thing that connects you to God, others, and self.

You can begin by asking and answering questions like this: *What was the most stressful thing you faced today? What is something you're excited about and why? How do you feel about ___________? How did you feel when I said that?* For some of you, this is going to take some insight to even stop and ask yourself what you might be feeling. If you need more help with the process of unpacking how you feel, I encourage you to put my book *Reset* on your reading list.

WHEN YOU COME FROM A FAMILY OF ORIGIN WHERE FEELINGS WEREN'T EXPRESSED, OR WORSE YET, THEY WERE IGNORED, STUFFED, OR COVERED UP, YOU START TO BELIEVE THAT EXPRESSING HOW YOU FEEL IS A SIGN OF WEAKNESS.

Feelings conversations are vulnerable, and they connect us to people in significant ways. So make sure you're hitting this depth at least daily in your most significant relationships and watch to see the change that begins to happen in your level of connection as your level of conversation deepens.

LEVEL 4 CONVERSATION: FAITH AND BELIEFS

I've been teaching the concept of the levels of conversations for a while, but it's only been in the past few years that I decided to add this fourth level of faith and beliefs. Because this type of conversation has always come naturally for me, I assumed it did for others too. But the more I work with people, the more I see how difficult it can be to talk about your faith and your beliefs and express your relationship with God to others. It makes sense. Your faith is a significant part of who you are. Your beliefs are often buried so deep down. Your interactions with God are so personal, and it can take courage to bring some of those things into your friendships and relationships.

But these things that are going on underneath the surface of your life are exactly what usher you into deeper relationships with others. Faith and beliefs conversations could be as simple as sharing something God is teaching you, or as complex as tapping into some of the underlying beliefs you struggle with, such as: *I'm not good enough.* What do you really believe about God, self, and others? And how do those beliefs inform and shape your life? There is a deep spiritual intimacy that comes with sharing some of these things out loud, and with that said, I believe there should be caution regarding whom we choose to share with. Scripture reminds us not to throw our pearls to pigs (Matthew 7:6), meaning we need to be careful to give the depths of ourselves to people who are responsible enough to hold our inner world with care.

Here are some questions to consider as you're trying to pave the way for level 4 conversations: *What is something God is teaching you? What is a belief you have about yourself that tends to keep you stuck? How can I be praying for you? What is something you believe about God and where did that belief come from?*

Let me leave you with this question as you think through the four levels of conversation and how they relate to your people skills: How deep are you? Because the answer to this will either propel you into deeper relationships or prevent you from getting there.

TAKE OWNERSHIP

1. Which of the four levels of conversation were most expressed in your family of origin? Which were not expressed? How has this impacted your personal conversation and communication as an adult?

2. On a scale of zero to ten (zero being totally uncomfortable and ten being very comfortable) what is your comfort level with each of the four levels of conversation?

   - Level 1: Facts ____
   - Level 2: Ideas and Opinions ____
   - Level 3: Feelings _____
   - Level 4: Faith and Beliefs _____

   Why do you think this is?

3. Write out three feelings you experienced in the last two weeks. Whom have you shared these feelings with?

4. Are there any relationships in which you need to be more intentional with going deeper in your level of conversations? If so, which relationships?

6

TELL THAT TO YOUR FACE

Body Language Matters

Every now and again I hear something so unexpected in a counseling session that I have to try really hard not to laugh out loud. This was one of those days. I was working with a married couple who were having some serious communication issues. The husband claimed that his wife often looked angry, frustrated, or irritated, but whenever he confronted her about what was wrong, she was adamant everything was fine. They were processing this pattern out loud in our session, and the wife was defensively explaining that she was genuinely not feeling the way her husband was interpreting, when he turned to her and said out loud with exasperation, "Well, then tell that to your face!"

Touché, I thought to myself. I mean, it was a pretty accurate comment. And I believe he was really on to something. I had them stop for a moment and asked him to explain what her face was telling him during these moments of misinterpretation. As he explained, she was sincerely surprised by the way he was describing her body language and had no awareness of how she may have been coming across without intending to. She wasn't feeling negative toward her husband, but her body language was communicating a different story.

It's been said that over 50 percent of our communication is conveyed by our body language.[1] I tend not to put too much weight on such vague statistics, but from experience both inside and outside of the counseling office, I do believe that our body language communicates and conveys a significant amount with or without our awareness.

OUR BODY LANGUAGE COMMUNICATES AND CONVEYS A SIGNIFICANT AMOUNT WITH OR WITHOUT OUR AWARENESS.

Let me ask you this: Why is it that some people just look friendly and inviting, while others don't? What makes the difference before you even speak to someone is their body language. It's called *open* body language versus *closed* body language. Open body language communicates kindness, interest, warmth, and welcome, whereas closed body language communicates discomfort, disinterest, apathy, irritability, or even aggression. We learn a lot about body language in counseling school, because how you come across when someone walks into your office or meets you for the first time (or even after ten years of marriage like the couple in the story!) matters significantly in the rapport and relationship you want to build.

Here are some things to consider about what your body language might be communicating that you may not even realize.

Arms: Open body language means that your arms are hanging comfortably by your body (depicting a safe stance) not crossed (depicting a protective stance). Relaxed arms communicate safety, security, and welcome, whereas rigid arms communicate discomfort and being in a state of high alert.

Face: Open body language in your face means your eyebrows are raised and not furrowed, your forehead is relaxed and not wrinkled, and your lips are relaxed and not tightly pressed together. Muscle tension is indicative of someone who is in fight-or-flight mode, and since your face muscles are the ones people see first, tense facial expressions can be interpreted as threatening rather than welcoming.

Eye contact: Looking someone directly in the eyes communicates focus and priority and makes them feel heard. Eye contact conveys that you really see them, rather than looking around or looking past them. But take note that proper eye contact doesn't mean staring them down without blinking, as that could come across as aggressive or even awkward, rather than welcoming. Aim for four to five seconds of eye contact at a time before looking away briefly.

Smiling: Take inventory of your resting face (grab a mirror for this part!) and analyze how you look when you're smiling, when you're frowning, as well as what your facial expressions look like in a neutral position. When engaging in a conversation with someone, it often takes intention to open your body language toward a simple smile rather than a neutral resting pose that may be misinterpreted. The simple gesture of smiling can communicate so much to the recipient of that smile. And it's true what they say: Smiling is contagious! (We'll learn more about mirror neurons in a later chapter.)

Hands: Open body language means your hands are open and relaxed rather than making closed fists, clasped together with interlaced fingers, or by your side. A leadership article by *Forbes* shows that people who talk with their hands tend to be viewed more positively than those who don't, and that those who use their hands to speak come across as more "warm, agreeable and energetic," while those who keep their hands still are seen as "logical, cold, and analytic."[2] Additionally, when your hands are visible, it communicates safety and security, whereas hidden hands (in your pockets or behind your back) may convey that you're trying to hide something or make you appear untrustworthy.

Distance: Open body language means keeping a close but comfortable distance when someone is talking to you, rather than standing extremely far away, which communicates discomfort and disinterest. Proximity matters because standing too far away can be just as off-putting to someone as standing too close within their kinetic sphere. I'm sure you've experienced that time when someone was a little too close to your face as they were talking, and how uncomfortable it likely felt. Respecting people's personal space, while standing close enough to communicate interest and comfort is an important part of unspoken body language.

Fidgeting: Be aware of your nervous energy. So many people exude this type of energy without even realizing they're doing it. Things like tapping on something with your fingers, shaking your leg or foot, twiddling your fingers, playing with your hair, shifting in place, or touching your face can be very distracting to the other person. Not only that, but nervous energy can also come across as a lack of interest, boredom, or impatience, even if you're genuinely not feeling any of those things.

If you've never taken inventory of your body language, I think today is the day to start. I challenge you to stand in front of a full-length mirror and take a little assessment of your body language and what you might be communicating. As awkward as this may feel, try communicating different expressions in front of a mirror and re-enact what you want to look like in different scenarios such as when you're meeting someone for the first time, walking into a room of people, confronting someone about something, or being confronted yourself. Observe your resting face, as well as how you express different moods and emotions. Try to objectively assess how your face and body language comes across and what you might want to tweak and adjust. It's better to be awkward for a little while in front of a mirror by yourself than it is to be awkward in your real-life relationships without awareness of how you're coming across. In addition, be aware of your body language over the next few days as you're interacting with people in real-life scenarios and try to get a feel of what your body language may be conveying.

I may not be as blunt as my client who told his wife to "tell that to your face," but I often take time to talk through body language with many of my clients, especially those who may be coming across as closed in their demeanor. Most of the time, confronting them and challenging them to assess their own body language and facial expressions is a first for them, something they weren't aware of until I mentioned it. And those small changes have made big differences in how they come across.

What is it that you want to communicate to the world around you? Whatever it is, be sure to tell that to your face.

TAKE OWNERSHIP

1. Take five minutes to stand in front of a full-length mirror. Practice expressing yourself by reenacting the following scenarios:

    a. Meeting someone for the first time.

    b. Greeting someone familiar you see while out and about.

    c. Walking into a social setting.

    d. Listening to someone confront you.

    e. Listening to someone who is sharing something important with you.

    f. Confronting someone.

    Take some time to observe how you physically express these moods and emotions: sadness, anger, interest, frustration, irritation, and a neutral resting face. Make observations about your body language and facial expressions and what you would like to change, adjust, or work on.

2. Does your body language communicate open or closed posture? Take time to review each of the categories of body language listed in this chapter and assess. How do you think your current body language may be interpreted by others?

3. Which category of body language or facial expression could you be more intentional with?

4. Ask a couple of people who are close to you to give you feedback regarding your body language and facial expressions and how you may come across.

7

POSITIVE AFFIRMATION

Making Deposits Before Withdrawals

Have you ever shown affirmation and appreciation to someone for simply passing the salt? There's a psychologist by the name of Russel Barkley (not to be confused with Charles Barkley; I was a hardcore Phoenix Suns fan back in the days of NBA glory) who specializes in helping parents with behavior modification strategies for extremely difficult children. He has an incredible eight-part program in which he teaches parents a step-by-step approach to achieving lasting behavior change in complex cases of both children and adolescents.[1] The eight parts of the program are staggered, meaning you're meant to spend a few weeks on each one before moving on to the next one. I remember sitting down with exasperated and exhausted parents, who were often looking for a quick fix, and introducing them to the eight parts of the program. Not surprisingly, many of them would give me a questioning look when I introduced the first stage: positive affirmation.

"Positive affirmation?" they would question. "We were hoping for something a little more practical," like a list of rules and consequences, a behavior modification plan, or even a magic wand. "Trust me," I would say. "This is where we need to start." The first part of the plan focuses the attention on positive affirmation as the primary means of building relationship and trust, which in turn, sets the foundation for behavior change.

Some would ask, "But what am I supposed to positively affirm when my child is displaying disobedience and bad behavior 99 percent of the time?"

I would respond, "Ask them for things you don't really need them to do—for example, passing the salt at the dinner table—and then affirm them for responding in a helpful way."

Could you please pass the salt?

It's such a basic request, but ultimately, it's not about the request at all, is it? The reason you start by asking your child to do things you don't really need done is because there's no consequence if they don't do it, but there is a reward if they do: the reward of positive affirmation. It's about creating an opportunity to fill the most powerful human need: the need to be affirmed. The need to be noticed, appreciated, valued, and positively reinforced. The need for someone to see the good in you and to call it out. We all have that need deep down, don't we? Whether we're a 12-year-old boy or a 62-year-old man. Whether we're a young teenage girl or a 45-year-old mom of four kids. We're made for love, and we're wired for affirmation.

Affirmation and appreciation are some of the most powerful tools we have in relationships, yet they are without a doubt the most underrated and underused. We often start out affirming people when they enter the world as tiny human beings, but somewhere along the way we grow numb to the need to continue that affirmation as the relationship grows and evolves. I have a memory of hooting and hollering and singing praises to my first-born baby when she would give a good big burp after drinking her bottle. "What a good girl! That was a great burp! You are Momma's pride and joy!" Everything she did, whether a smile or the passing of gas (burp or otherwise), was worthy of affirmation. Now that she's fourteen, it's so much easier to overlook her day-to-day need for positive affirmation, even though deep down she's still my baby girl! (She was sitting in front of me at a coffee shop, working on her homework for Spanish class, while I wrote this chapter. I took my own advice and stopped to tell her how special she is, how proud I am of her, and how much she means to me. Her face absolutely lit up when I did. Let's never take for granted the power of sharing what's in our hearts with the people we love the most and calling out all that is good!) The power of positive affirmation matters whether you're four months old, 14 years old, or 94 years old.

AFFIRMATION AND APPRECIATION ARE SOME OF THE MOST POWERFUL TOOLS WE HAVE IN RELATIONSHIPS, YET THEY ARE WITHOUT A DOUBT THE MOST UNDERRATED AND UNDERUSED.

And consider this: How much more do we neglect the giving of praise, appreciation, and affirmation in our everyday relationships with our spouse, our families, our children, our colleagues, and our community? In fact, I believe we're a culture that is starved of genuine appreciation and affirmation. And when we don't get the affirmation we desire from the people we love and trust, we'll often go to great lengths to find it from others, those who may not be as loving or as trustworthy. There is power in seeing one another, and in calling out the God-given, innate value inside of each of us.

DEPOSITS BEFORE WITHDRAWALS

Back to the eight-part behavior plan. The big idea behind starting the plan with positive affirmation is to fill the emotional account with affirmation before you deplete it with correction. And the most fascinating thing about this plan is that I have had *so many* parents come back to me after the first two weeks of applying only this first part of the plan to say that they've seen extraordinary changes in their child's behavior. That's because positive affirmation paves the way for impact and influence in any relationship. It is more powerful than any correction or behavior modification tool. It's more effective than guilt-trips, threats, bribes, or coercion.

This doesn't just apply to children; this applies to people of all ages and stages of life. I find myself repeating these principles over and over again in everything from marriage counseling to staff and leadership trainings. You have to make deposits before you take withdrawals. If we treat our relationships like a bank account, it makes financial sense that you can't withdraw money if there's nothing in the account to begin with. But so often we go about our relationships with that skewed mentality. We try to withdraw from the account by asking for change, offering corrections or criticisms, requesting our needs to be met, making uninvited suggestions, asking for favors, or trying to engage in difficult conversations before we've spent the proper time making the emotional deposits. And this is not a one-to-one ratio. One deposit doesn't equal one withdrawal. In fact, modern counseling encourages people to offer three to five affirmations before offering one suggestion or correction.

If we're honest with ourselves, most of us are really far away from hitting that goal. Not because of a lack of opportunity, but because of a lack of intentionality. I've heard it said that we starve people of affirmation, but we wouldn't starve them of food. We're quick to offer our corrections and observations, and slow to offer our appreciation and affirmations. Or, just as bad, we simply stay in neutral territory hoping that will get us through. We refrain from offering both affirmation and requests. We neither deposit nor withdraw. But in doing so, we miss out on the beauty of connection and the deep intimacy of relationships. We miss out on the impact and influence we could have on those around us. Ephesians 4:29 reminds us of the importance and power of this concept when it says, "Do not let any unwholesome talk come out of your mouths, but only what is helpful for building others up according to their needs, that it may benefit those who listen." We have the opportunity and the responsibility to build each other up by how we speak. We're invited to speak in a way that benefits others by the intentional words that come out of our mouths.

WE'RE QUICK TO OFFER OUR CORRECTIONS AND OBSERVATIONS, AND SLOW TO OFFER OUR APPRECIATION AND AFFIRMATIONS.

Whether you're interacting with one of your children, your spouse, or a coworker, whether you're navigating a relationship with someone who would be considered difficult or just another daily interaction, ask yourself: are you making deposits? Are you leaving them with the gift of feeling seen, noticed, appreciated, and affirmed? Are you making the most of the powerful tool of positive affirmation? If you can answer yes, you'll start to see extraordinary changes in your relationships. Be intentional with the positive affirmation you give this week and watch what a little intentionality can do for your relationships.

TAKE OWNERSHIP

1. Are you the type of person who typically offers correction or affirmation? Why?

2. Consider the three-to-one ratio (three deposits for one withdrawal). How can you be intentional with your positive affirmations today?

3. What was the atmosphere of positive affirmation (or lack thereof) in your family of origin? How do you think this impacted your intentionality with positive affirmation?

4. Consider one relationship in your life that needs the deposit of positive affirmation. What are some things you can begin to affirm?

5. Make a list of two separate categories: Affirmations for what they *do* (You're really gifted with organization, You're a great planner, I appreciate the energy you spent on this

particular task, etc.) and affirmations about who they *are* (You're such a generous person, I appreciate your sense of humor, I'm so grateful you're in my life, I appreciate your creativity, You're so considerate and thoughtful, etc). Write down some affirmations in both categories that you can begin to express today. Observe how it impacts the relationship as you make a steady habit of positive affirmation.

8

EMPATHY IS EVERYTHING

Looking Out Their Window

There's a popular book that's required reading for most counselors in training called *The Gift of Therapy*, by Irvin Yalom. In this little book he offers lessons for young counselors reminding them that it's a gift to be a therapist and instructing them on how to do it well. In one chapter he talks about the power of empathy and being able to see life from our client's perspective. This lesson has stayed with me, and I believe it's a lesson that applies to how we interact with everyone who comes our way.

He shares a story about a woman who had been at odds with her naysaying father for many years. They could never see eye to eye, and their relationship was strained. She was looking forward to the opportunity of having him drive her home from college so they could connect. But the entire drive home, all he talked about was the ugly, garbage-filled creek on the side of the road. She couldn't understand because all she saw was a beautiful, rustic creek. She felt discouraged by his attitude, so she shut down. Years later, after her father had passed, she was making that same drive home, this time as the driver, and to her surprise she noticed that there were two creeks. The one that was originally out her father's window was as ugly and garbage littered as he had observed. But by the time she had learned to look out his window, it was too late. Her father had already passed.

This story stuck with me to the point that I still remember it 25 years later. And not just for how I interact with my clients, but how I interact with people in everyday life. Empathy is everything. The opportunity to really challenge myself to look out someone else's window and see life through their eyes even when they are doing something hurtful or unkind. Even when they are acting in a way that I don't understand or appreciate.

I interact with so many clients who have been hurt by someone. In fact, I can't think of one client I know who *hasn't* been hurt by someone. But why do some people allow the hurt from others to cause bitterness and resentment while others don't? Why do some people allow their wounds and pain to shut them off from the world, while others continue to trust and connect and try again? The answer is empathy. I believe empathy is the only way we can truly lean into the hope of healthy relationships. Not only that, I believe it's the only way we can truly forgive when we've been hurt.

I was recently talking about this with one of my clients, who was having a really hard time letting go of some of the hurts from her childhood. During our session, the Lord gave me a picture of Jesus, hanging on a cross saying, "Father, forgive them for they know not what they do" (Luke 23:34 ESV). The second part of that beautiful phrase uttered from the lips of Jesus Himself is filled with *empathy*. He was able to forgive because He looked out the window from the perspective of those who were hurting Him, and realized they were coming from a place of ignorance, a deficit of knowledge, and a lack of understanding. They had no idea what they were doing.

They were blind, confused, and shrouded in darkness. "*They know not what they do.*"

I think sometimes trauma does something similar. It clouds our vision, confuses our steps, taints our behaviors, and shrouds our life with darkness. I think of the people who have deeply hurt me, and the people who have hurt you, and I wonder if we would have the courage to see life from their vantage point: the garbage-littered creek that they are faced with, that we may know nothing about. I wonder if the only way out of the pain in our own lives is to begin to see the pain in the lives of others. Not as an excuse, *never* as an excuse, but as an entry point—a path for us to move through the pain, and hurt, and betrayal through the window of empathy.

I WONDER IF THE ONLY WAY OUT OF THE PAIN IN OUR OWN LIVES IS TO BEGIN TO SEE THE PAIN IN THE LIVES OF OTHERS.

SUPERFICIAL OR SIGNIFICANT

I wonder what changes we would see in our feelings and behaviors in our interpersonal relationships if we chose empathy as our first response. How would it change our interactions with the grumpy waitress, if we could only see out her window as a single mom trying to care for three children. How would it change our reaction to our boss if we could see out his window to the marriage conflicts and struggles he faced that morning as his wife dropped the word *divorce*. How would it change our heart toward our spouse, if we could see out their window and discover how childhood hurt and shame get reactivated when we offer them correction or critique? How would it change our approach to our children, if we could see out their window and find they're facing a problem they desperately need help to navigate?

How would it change our perspective on the people who have hurt, betrayed, and caused us pain if we could get a glimpse of the pain they carry? I don't know the answer to that, but I do know the astronomical difference it's made in my own life as I'm navigating pain in this specific season of life and tending to some deep wounds that others have caused me. Being able to look through the window of empathy has softened my heart. Having empathy for the pain of those who have caused me pain has changed me. Empathy has been everything. The perspectives it's shifted. The healing it's brought. The forgiveness it's conducted. And the relationships it's fostered as a result.

Whether it's a superficial hurt or a significant one, empathy allows us to get a different perspective, and in doing so, it allows us to have a different reaction. When we can understand why a person may have done what they've done, where they may be coming from, and the burdens they might be carrying, we can often choose to navigate our response in a healthier and more productive way. Whose window do you need to look out of today as you navigate difficult relationships and situations? Whose window do you need to look out today as you tend to the pain, bitterness, and resentment in your own heart? Whose window do you need to look out of today as you take steps toward the entry point of forgiveness and freedom? I know the hurt is deep. And I am praying that the healing is even deeper. In Jesus's name.

WHETHER IT'S A SUPERFICIAL HURT OR A SIGNIFICANT ONE, EMPATHY ALLOWS US TO GET A DIFFERENT PERSPECTIVE, AND IN DOING SO, IT ALLOWS US TO HAVE A DIFFERENT REACTION.

TAKE OWNERSHIP

1. When it comes to empathy, rate yourself on a scale of your tendency to look out the other's window (zero being I always think about my perspective first and ten being I always consider the other person's perspective first). ______________. What about in relationships where you have been hurt? ________________.

2. What is a hurt from the past that you have struggled to let go of? Why has that been difficult?

3. How can you use empathy to try to begin shifting your perspective and finding deeper healing?

4. What is your reaction when you think of Jesus's practicing empathy as a pathway to forgiveness while dying on the cross (Luke 23:34)?

9

WHAT'S YOUR TYPE?

Own Your Communication Style

Imagine you just arrived at a much-anticipated dining experience at a brand-new restaurant that everyone's been talking about. You've been planning this for months because the restaurant has been booked for that long, and you were finally able to get your highly coveted reservation. You sit down with your party, place your orders, and small talk with one another while you wait for the grand entrance of your meal. After a little wait, you see the waiter coming out with your table's orders. He starts to set the plates down in front of each person and finally gets to yours. He sets down your plate in front of you, and at a quick glance, you notice your order actually came out wrong.

What would you do?

Are you the type of person who would most likely bring it to the attention of the waiter right away and ask for it to be fixed, changed, or altered?

Are you the type of person who wouldn't make a big deal about it out loud, but then you'd remain internally bothered by the mistake throughout the rest of the meal?

Are you the type of person who would choose not to mention it because you don't want to make a fuss, and just deal with it as long as it's generally edible?

Or are you the type of person who would make sure to bring attention to it, demand that it be changed right away, and then expect or even pressure the restaurant to go the next step by comping your meal or giving you a discount to make up for the inconvenience?

Generally, when it comes to communication styles there are four distinct types of communicators: passive, assertive, aggressive, and passive-aggressive (hopefully you can identify which one is which in the examples above). And even though what you do at a restaurant is just a small example of your communication type, it often reflects the overall picture of the type of communicator you are. These unique communication styles have a huge effect on your people skills, as well as how you come across to the world around you. Let's talk a little more about each one.

COMMUNICATION STYLES

Passive Communication Style

Passive communicators are generally more inclined to think of others and how they will think or feel and what they might need, rather than consider their own thoughts, feelings, and needs. In the restaurant example, a passive person may think, "I don't want to burden the waitress. She seems busy and stressed. And this isn't a big deal, so I can deal with it" (even if they got a totally different meal than they ordered). This communication style is usually fueled by a hyper awareness of what others need and a muted awareness of your own personal needs and emotions.

There are many reasons people develop a passive communication style, but most often it comes from patterns of development in your family of origin. For instance, maybe you grew up in a family dynamic where someone else had higher needs than you. Maybe there was a sibling who had a disability, or significant rebellion issues, or some sort of mental health illness. Maybe mom and dad were always in conflict. Maybe there was financial strain or family stress or something else that made the needs of those around you feel so much bigger than your own needs. In that context, it becomes easy to simply tell yourself that there is no room for your needs, and so it's easier to just put your needs on the backburner. You learn to make your voice smaller and focus on those around you instead.

The problem with passive communication is that it refrains from sharing the full truth. It's a communication style that tends to hold back out of avoidance and fear: fear of conflict, fear of rejection, fear of what others might think, etc. Over time, passive communicators may struggle with feelings of bitterness or resentment, because their lack of emotional expression and inability to express their needs begin to build up underneath the surface. But God's Word encourages us to speak the truth in love, which means that we have a responsibility to be truth-tellers (Ephesians 4:15). You cannot be a passive communicator and a truth-teller at the same time. Like I said, there are many reasons why you can end up with a passive communication style, and it's important for each person to unpack some of their past to get to the root of their *why* in order to learn how to speak the truth in love.[1]

Aggressive Communication Style

On the flip side of this is the aggressive communicator. They're often in self-protection mode and can perceive even the smallest mistakes and grievances as attacks. They don't want to let others take advantage of them or hurt them in any way, so they make sure to make it a point to assert what they want and how they want it. Often, this can come across as intense, bossy, aggressive, rude, and even threatening to those listening. It could be communication about something as benign and simple as "my burger is well-done instead of medium," but the communication comes across as "you-against-me" rather than "how can we resolve this together?"

Aggressive communicators often come from a background of pain, hurt, abandonment, or rejection. They were genuinely wounded at some point in their life, and so their hyper-vigilance became their self-protective mode. They are constantly scanning their environment for who and what could hurt them, wanting to deal with it before it deals with them. Whether superficial or significant things, aggressive communicators lump it all in a similar category and have the mindset that *you're either against me or you're with me.*

The problem with aggressive communicators is that, though they get what they want, it's often at the expense of hurt feelings, strained relationships, misunderstandings, and a pattern of conflict and broken relationships along the way. Their aggressive style ends up building a wall around them, keeping people out—whether or not that's their intention. They end up feeling isolated, alone, and even misunderstood. Proverbs 15:1 is clear that "a soft answer turns away wrath, but a harsh word stirs up anger" (ESV). Aggressive communication style ends up leading to anger and frustration, pushing others away rather than bringing them close. You may end up getting everything you *want,* but you also end up getting nothing you actually *need* because you find yourself living in emotional isolation.

YOU MAY END UP GETTING EVERYTHING YOU *WANT,* BUT YOU ALSO END UP GETTING NOTHING YOU ACTUALLY *NEED* BECAUSE YOU FIND YOURSELF LIVING IN EMOTIONAL ISOLATION.

Passive-Aggressive Style

Then there's the passive-aggressive style of communication. This type of communicator appears passive externally but then reacts aggressively internally. For instance, if they were at a restaurant and their order came out wrong, they would accept it, but then they would complain to everyone at the table about why the order was wrong and why they dislike this restaurant. Or maybe they would stay quiet about it but have a negative mood for the rest of the night instead. Rather than being clear and direct with the waiter, they might give them the cold shoulder, respond with short, rude interactions, and then leave them a terrible tip at the end. They don't clearly articulate what they need, and then they act rude, childish, cold, or distant when people don't read their minds or give them what they want.

Many people with passive-aggressive communication styles come from past patterns of neglect or abandonment. They didn't feel safe enough or cared for enough, and they were unable to communicate what they needed or wanted. So they developed an unhealthy method of trying to communicate their needs in indirect, childish, immature, or manipulative ways.

The passive-aggressive communication style ends up with the worst of both worlds. Not only do they push people away through their immature behavior, but they also don't get their needs met because they weren't clear and direct with what they wanted. They end up feeling hurt, misunderstood, and unsatisfied internally, and isolated and alone externally. Matthew 5:37 is an important reminder to reign in our passive-aggressive nature, and be clear and direct with what we want or need. I love how the New Living Translation puts it: "Just say a simple, 'Yes, I will,' or 'No, I won't.' Anything beyond this is from the evil one." Upon first read, it might seem extreme to say that indirect communication is "from the evil one," but if you could sit in my counseling seat and begin to see how passive-aggressive, aggressive, and passive communication styles can begin to destroy relationships and wreak havoc on lives, you'd likely wholeheartedly agree.

Assertive Communication Style

This is the type of communication style we should all strive for. And not only that, I believe it's a communication style that reflects the heart of Jesus, who was so clear, direct, gracious, compassionate, and kind. Matthew 12:36 reminds us that we will literally be held accountable for every word that comes out of our mouths. If that's the case, then this is something we need to take seriously. Because in that case, it's much more than a communication style, it's a reflection of our intentions and motivations. It's a reflection of our hearts. Matthew 15:18 affirms this again when it says, "What comes out of the mouth proceeds from the heart" (ESV). A healthy communicator is intentional and deliberate with every word that comes out of their mouth. Proverbs 15:28 reminds us, "The heart of the righteous ponders how to answer" (ESV).

IT'S MUCH MORE THAN A COMMUNICATION STYLE; IT'S A REFLECTION OF OUR INTENTIONS AND MOTIVATIONS. IT'S A REFLECTION OF OUR HEARTS.

An assertive communication style means that you are intentional to say what you need in a respectful way. Rather than only focusing on what others need (passive style) or only focusing on what you need (aggressive style), assertive communicators have a mutually minded mentality. You can assess your personal needs, not at the expense of others, but as a collaboration with others. You are good at understanding your rights and setting boundaries to protect yourself, yet you can do this while communicating respectfully and kindly to others.

Even when faced with totally opposing viewpoints, assertive communicators are aware of the difference between mountains and molehills, and they'll pick and choose battles that are significant with the perspective of what will be the most beneficial in the long run. In the case of the restaurant, an assertive person can clearly communicate what is wrong and suggest how it can be made right in a firm but kind way. They don't feel flustered or intimidated when they communicate, and the people they are communicating with don't feel demeaned, bull-dozed, bossed around, or attacked. It's a collaborative approach where all parties are respected, but boundaries are still kept intact.

To be honest, most people struggle to stay in this type of assertive communication style because it takes intentionality and awareness: intentionality to communicate in a collaborative way, and awareness of our underlying issues (the *why* behind our communication style) that tend to push us toward unhealthy communication styles. But learning how to ask the hard questions and get to the root of our communication style can change everything.

Your communication style will either push you away from others, push others away from you, or keep you close and connected in meaningful relationships. So learn to check your heart, observe your communication style, and be intentional with the words that come out of your mouth. And then watch how it impacts your relationships.

TAKE OWNERSHIP

1. Which communication style do you generally lean toward: passive, aggressive, passive-aggressive, or assertive?

2. Do you have a different communication style depending on the issue at hand? What are some examples of this, and why might this be?

3. Name one area of your life where you need to practice being more assertive.

4. What are some factors from your childhood, past experiences, or family of origin that may have impacted your communication style? Where might God be challenging you to go back and find healing? Take some time to journal and process this question at length, or with the help of a counselor.[2]

10

LISTENING SKILLS

Fifty Percent Is a Failing Grade

I was taking a walk around our neighborhood with two of my kids recently when we ran into two neighbors we'd never officially met before. We stopped to chat and introduced ourselves. They shared their names (as well as the names of their two dogs that they were walking), and immediately after they shared their names the husband quickly said, "It's okay if you have to ask us again!"

I love a good challenge. And as soon as I heard him say that, I literally thought to myself: *There's no way I'm going to ask again, especially now that I know that he expects me to ask again!* I spent the next 20 seconds or so of our conversation using memory hacks to seal in their names. My husband had recently explained to me a memory hack he learned from a book that explained how you can link names to memorable objects in order to remember people's names, so I tried to lock them in using those mental strategies.[1] Meanwhile, I missed the next 20 seconds of conversation because I was engaged in the conversation externally but was actually thinking about ways to remember their names internally. Once I realized I had no idea where we were in conversation, I clicked back as fast as I could to what they were talking about and finished our brief conversation. Upon walking away, I instantly realized I had no idea what their names were. The mental olympics I was doing throughout our conversation left me mentally exhausted and with nothing to show for it! At least I remembered they had two dogs! So, he was right. I'm going to have to ask him again the next time I see them.

We've all had that moment when we're introduced to someone for the first time, and within literally seconds of hearing their names our minds go blank, and we totally forget their names. Like I said, there are lots of memory devices that may be able to help with this (*may* being the key word), but I think the more important thing to remember is that listening is a skill set more than it is a simple hack to remembering someone's name. Because on the flip side, someone might actually remember your name in a conversation (you can tell when they're trying to remember because they'll often say your name repeatedly while you're talking), yet still not have good listening skills in the conversation! The skill of really listening is not a hack; it's something you have to develop over a period of time and with intentionality. It's a people skill, and one of the most important ones too. Sadly, it's also the most underrated, underappreciated, and under practiced.

THE SKILL OF REALLY LISTENING IS NOT A HACK; IT'S SOMETHING YOU HAVE TO DEVELOP OVER A PERIOD OF TIME AND WITH INTENTIONALITY.

FIFTY PERCENT IS FAILING

If you think about it, listening skills account for at least 50 percent of your conversation, because they require you to be in tune to the information and communication that's being transmitted your way.

Your ability to receive that information and process it accurately makes or breaks the entire conversation. If you receive zero percent of the communication being transmitted your way in a conversation, for instance, you're left with only 50 percent of the content, which is what you communicated to the person in front of you (that's assuming you communicated *perfectly*). And let me put it to you simply: 50 percent is a failing grade.

If that's the reality, then why is it that we spend so much more time focused on how to communicate than how to listen? It's no wonder that James 1:19 starts with the skill of listening: "Everyone should be quick to listen, slow to speak." Quick to listen. I don't know if this phrase would describe too many of us, if we're completely honest. And the question is *why*? Why is it so hard for us to be good listeners? Why is listening usually the passive portion of our conversations rather than the active priority? My guess is that it's rooted in an underlying belief system (leave it to the counselor to always go there). I wonder if it's because deep down we actually believe what we're saying is somehow more important, valuable, or urgent than what the other person is saying. Deep down we believe that what we have to say is more important than what we have to hear. And belief systems really do go a long way.

DEEP DOWN WE BELIEVE THAT WHAT WE HAVE TO SAY IS MORE IMPORTANT THAN WHAT WE HAVE TO HEAR.

SHIFTING OUR BELIEFS

The opposite of believing that what you have to say is more important than what you have to hear isn't believing that what you have to say is *not* valuable, but it's choosing to believe that the communication of the person standing before you is *just* as valuable. Philippians 2:4 is an important affirmation of that mindset shift: "Let each of you look not only to his own interests, but also to the interests of others" (ESV). *Also* is the key word here. Don't be so focused on what you have to say, your own interests, ideas, and input, that you miss the interests of others. Their 50 percent is *just as important* as yours. In fact, it might even be considered more important conversationally in that if you miss it, you're back to a failing grade of 50 percent no matter how well, clear, or effective your own conversation skills were.

Whether you're talking to your spouse in a heated conversation or to your boss in an awkward one, your ability to receive their interests and input in the conversation is crucial to the outcome of the entire equation. If you struggle to believe this deep down, it's important to ask yourself why. Because of your past, some of you are in self-protective mode: afraid to let your guard down and truly consider the interests of others out of fear you'll get hurt, forgotten, neglected, or silenced if you don't speak up and speak out. I'm going to go back to this often throughout this book, but dealing with those underlying belief systems rooted in past "people wounds" is the first step in being able to build healthy people skills. So what are your underlying belief systems, and how do they show up in your listening skills?

RECLAIMING THE 50 PERCENT

Now that we've gotten to deeper motivations, let's come up for air and talk about some practical ways to strengthen your listening skills. Here's how you can reclaim the 50 percent of conversation that would otherwise get lost without your ability to receive it through listening.

Remove Distractions

Distractions are everywhere. It's easy for your listening to get hijacked, not because of a lack of motivation, but simply because of distraction. Make it a point to put away your phone, turn off the TV or music, and limit distractions as you're able when you're involved in a conversation. My husband knows he has a tendency to be easily distracted, so when we're on a date, he makes it a point to choose the seat that has the least amount of stimulation (away from doors or spots where people are walking in and out, facing away from TVs and other screens, etc.) so he can stay focused on tuning out the external stimuli and tuning into our conversation.

Practice Active Listening

Active listening is the body language we portray during a conversation. When we're engaged in really listening to someone, believing that what they have to say is *just* as important, our body language and tone should match that belief. When you're listening to someone speak, be intentional about looking them in the eyes, nod your head to show that you're receiving the content, and use follow-up questions to clarify or comments that stay on track and elaborate what the person is saying. Not only does this help the other person know you're listening, but this active engagement also helps you to stay tuned in to what's being said. Active listening goes a long way in my counseling office, and it will go a long way in your interactions as well.

Don't Interrupt

I have a list of three pet peeves, and this is one of them. Be careful not to interrupt or interject when you're listening to someone. Wait until they finish their sentence or thought process before you jump in to reply. Interrupting someone is a telltale sign of a lack of listening skills, because you're often so focused on what you want to say next that you jump in before the right time rather than stilling your own thoughts enough to receive what's being said to you. So take note of your tendency to interrupt and work on truly listening.

Use Reflection

If I had to narrow listening skills down to one trait, it would be this one. Reflection is the ability to repeat back (in your own words) what the other person is saying in order to make them feel heard. In fact, it's such an important part of listening that it's one of the pillars of a proven marriage communication activity called the *Speaker Listener Technique*.[2] The goal of reflection is to receive and then process what the other person is saying, and then communicate to them that it's been received by offering them a short summary of what you believe they said. The goal isn't to simply parrot the person talking, meaning you don't want to repeat what they told you verbatim. The goal is to listen and learn. For example, someone might say, "Today was rough. My car broke down on the way to work, my boss called an unexpected meeting to offer me feedback, and I didn't have time for lunch, so I had to hit up the vending machines." To which an active listener might respond, "I'm so sorry, it sounds like you had a really frustrating day where everything that could go wrong pretty much did." You could also start a reflective sentence by saying something like, "What I'm hearing you say is that..." and reflect back what you've heard in your own words.

Reflection is powerful because it not only requires you to actually listen and learn, but it also communicates to the person speaking that you're truly present and engaged in what they're saying. I don't take it lightly when I say that the skill of reflection could literally change your relationships.

As I'm writing this chapter, I realize that I could commit an entire book to the subject of listening. And maybe you're reading this and realizing you could probably use a whole book about it. Maybe that's your next step. But for now, take inventory of your belief systems, try these practical strategies, and see if you can make a dent in that 50 percent.

TAKE OWNERSHIP

1. Have you ever thought about listening in terms of 50 percent of communication? What is your reaction to that concept?

2. On a scale of zero to ten (zero being the poorest listening skills), what number would you rate yourself on listening skills?

3. What is your underlying belief system about the importance of looking at the interests of others (as portrayed in Philippians 2:4)? Where do you think this belief system came from?

4. Which of the four listening strategies (remove distraction, practice active listening, don't interrupt, use reflection) do you struggle with the most? How can you implement one of these strategies a little more this week?

11

BE REAL

Authenticity Attracts

Every now and again when my brother comes to visit for the weekend, he'll stop and give me a quick heads up that I'm about to be a part of his *BeReal* photo. You may have heard of it, or even use it yourself, but *BeReal* is an app with the goal of authenticity. It encourages you to stop whatever you're doing when the daily prompt goes off in order to *BeReal*, by taking a photo that captures yourself in selfie-form as well as whatever is happening on the other side of the camera and then sends that double-sided picture to your friends. Each day you get the prompt to *BeReal* at a different time, and the spontaneity of it encourages everyone on the app to share their regular moments of life. It's meant to give your friends and followers a candid, unscripted, uncurated, genuine glimpse into your everyday real life in contrast to the perfectly framed photos you often find on Instagram.

I can't say I ever got into this trend, and I probably never will because, if I'm honest, I find it rather intrusive. I'd prefer to post on social media in my own time and in my own way. That probably tells you more about my personality than it does about the app itself. But there's something about the popularity of this app that hits the core of our desire as human beings: We want to know others and be known in a genuine and authentic way. There's something about authenticity that's attractive.

Unfortunately, the culture of most social media platforms has made authenticity really difficult. Because everything is so perfectly curated online, we tend to fall into the trap of putting filters over our lives, presenting things in the way we want them to appear or the way we think others expect us to appear rather than in the way they really are. We choose aesthetics over authenticity. I think most of us fall into this trap on a regular basis. And if we're not careful, it begins to spill over into how we do real-life relationships as well because a lack of authenticity begins to inhibit authentic connections and relationships. You can't be truly known and truly loved if you're not willing to present the true you.

YOU CAN'T BE TRULY KNOWN AND TRULY LOVED IF YOU'RE NOT WILLING TO PRESENT THE TRUE YOU.

KNOW YOURSELF

While I don't believe the ultimate answer to authenticity means taking candid photos of yourself and posting them on social media, I do believe the answer is to work toward being truly known. But before you can be truly known by others, you have to first be truly known by yourself. Some of you are probably in the very beginning of the journey of self-awareness and self-insight. You're learning about your underlying beliefs, taking inventory of your thoughts, owning your emotions, and discovering patterns for why you do what you do.[1] Others of you have been on this journey for a while and have a deeper understanding of what makes you who you are as well as what you're about. The journey of self-awareness is regularly looking inward and involves understanding how your past has shaped your present, being aware of your strengths and weaknesses, understanding the intricacies of your personality, and staying in tune to your underlying motivations. If I had to summarize this process of self-awareness with one verse, I'd choose Proverbs 20:5, which reminds us that the purposes of a person's heart are like deep waters, but a person of insight can draw out those waters. Knowing ourselves is the journey of drawing out that water from the depths of who we are. It takes time, effort, energy, and intentionality.

SHARE YOURSELF

If knowing yourself is drawing out the deep waters, then sharing yourself means giving others that water to drink. It's not enough just to know yourself, being authentic means you share what you learn and know about yourself with others. Authenticity is your way of genuinely connecting with the people around you, giving them a glimpse of who you really are and what's going on inside of you. It's allowing others to see both your highlights and lowlights, your strengths and weaknesses, your victories and struggles, your triumphs and failures. It's about letting people in. It's about taking off the filter. It's about seeing authenticity as the way you truly connect, because it's only when you're truly known that you can be truly loved.

WHO KNOWS?

I'm not saying you need to have total authenticity on your social media platforms (although I do think a little authenticity goes a long way). In fact, I am extra careful on social media because I have to be able to trust you in order to let you in, and when it comes to a public social media platform, it's impossible to get to that level. But what I am saying is that you need to start taking inventory of your real-life relationships and how authentic and genuine you are with the people you desire to stay connected to and build intimacy with. This includes your spouse, your children, your family, and your friends. Who really knows you? Who are you intentionally sharing your life with? Do you make it a point to share both highs and lows with the people you care about the most? Is there anything in your life that you've kept a secret, something that no one knows? What prevents you from sharing your authentic self with those you love?

At the end of the day, full authenticity really comes down to an ability to trust like I mentioned before. You have to truly trust someone in order to let them in, but if there's *no one* you trust, then the trust issue might have something to do with *you*. Trust doesn't require someone to have a 100 percent perfect track record (otherwise no one would have a chance), but it does require us to believe that they are 100 percent in our corner: they love us unconditionally and care for us completely. It's less about perfection and more about commitment. Sometimes we struggle to trust because we're in a relationship where trust has been broken; other times we struggle to trust because of broken trust from our past. But both cases require us to do some healing in order for us to be able to move forward in authentic relationships. Let's spend some time assessing where we are with trust, self-awareness, and authenticity. Because in order to be truly loved, we have to be truly known. And in order to be truly known, we have to learn to be real.

IT'S LESS ABOUT PERFECTION AND MORE ABOUT COMMITMENT.

TAKE OWNERSHIP

1. When it comes to trust, when has trust been broken for you and how has that had a ripple effect on your relationships? Is there something in your life that no one knows about? If so, why is that?

2. Do you take regular time to know yourself? If yes, what do those practices look like in your day-to-day life? If no, what are some ways you can begin engaging in that process?

3. Do you find that your tendency to be filtered begins to seep into your real-life relationships? How so?

4. Who are the people in your life you can be real with? Who are the people in your life you need to be more intentionally authentic with?

12

VULNERABILITY LEADS TO INTIMACY

The Pratfall Effect

Did you know that your weaknesses and mistakes can actually make you more likeable? Don't believe me? What if I told you that science confirms it? Psychologist Elliot Aronson conducted a significant social experiment in the 1960s called the Pratfall Effect, in which he discovered that highly competent individuals were actually rated much more likeable by their audience when they showed some sort of weakness through a blunder or mistake (the word *pratfall* actually means a humiliating or embarrassing mistake). The more polished or perfect they appeared, the less they were liked. I find this especially fascinating because we live in a culture that wants us to believe that perfection is the way to people's hearts, when in fact, it's often the exact opposite. It's an incredible phenomenon that I believe holds true in everyday interactions as well. There's something about our weaknesses that connects us to other human beings.

WE LIVE IN A CULTURE THAT WANTS US TO BELIEVE THAT PERFECTION IS THE WAY TO PEOPLE'S HEARTS, WHEN IN FACT, IT'S OFTEN THE EXACT OPPOSITE.

People want to feel like they can relate to us. Perfection is intimidating because if you think about it, it's really hard to measure up to (*hello*, no one is actually perfect), and so it begins to set up a psychological barrier of comparison in the people we're interacting with. The more perfect and flawless a person comes across, the less people feel that they're able to connect and relate to that person. It's almost like a perceived wall that keeps people away and inhibits them from truly connecting. But when they begin to see and feel a person's humanity through their mistakes or weaknesses, things begin to shift relationally.

THE WALL OF PERFECTION

I believe the reason that showing weakness is hard for so many people is because we fall into the trap of believing that being perfect and polished is the way to be loved. Often, that faulty belief system comes from our past. Maybe you grew up in a family where perfection was demanded or required in order to feel approval and love from your parents or caregivers. Maybe you grew up in an environment where mistakes were not allowed, and there would be severe punishment or consequences if you didn't measure up to a certain standard. Maybe you experienced an environment of abuse or bullying, where your weaknesses were preyed upon by others and used to hurt you rather than help you. These experiences shape our belief systems, and in turn our behaviors. They shape our ability to either let our walls down and let people in, or choose to keep up the appearance of perfection.

I counseled a young woman who was bullied throughout her childhood. She had some mild disabilities and struggles from birth that drew negative attention from immature and unrelenting middle schoolers. She was picked on, bullied, and tormented for many years. Add to that, she grew up in a culture where a high standard was demanded by her parents, despite her genuine setbacks and struggles. Fast forward 15 years and she's now one of the most flawless young adult women I've ever met. If you were to look her up on Instagram, you'd find the most picture-perfect person, with not a flaw in sight. Her makeup is perfect, her outfits are fashionable, her backgrounds are picturesque, and her social media posts are perfectly scripted out. In fact, our first counseling session felt more like a perfect audition rather than a conversation. The problem is, she's having a really hard time connecting in the world of dating. Her perfection is keeping people away. One gentleman she dated even told her directly that she's just too polished to the point where he doesn't feel like he can connect with her. The very same coping mechanisms that served her in one season of life (the need to be perfect) are sabotaging her in this season of life.

VULNERABILITY LEADS TO INTIMACY

This is where the power of vulnerability comes in. Vulnerability is the ability to be vulnerable: to share your weaknesses, struggles, deficits, and failures in an intentional way with the people you want to connect with. It's choosing not to hide behind the wall of perceived perfection. You don't have to trip over your feet or have an embarrassing moment just to be liked, but you do have to be intentionally vulnerable and let people in. Vulnerability offers a doorway into the wall of perfection and invites people to see the real you: the parts of you that they can connect with and relate to. I know that some of you hear the word vulnerability and probably cringe because you've perceived it to be a weakness or an emotional explosion of some sort. But I promise you, it's the key to intimacy. It takes our relationships to new levels of connection. You can't get to intimacy without vulnerability.

Is it risky? Yes, sometimes it is. Because the people whom you invite in are the same people who can hurt you. This is why it's important to assess whom we're vulnerable with and how much vulnerability we choose to have. The closer the relationship, the higher the level of vulnerability should be.

HOW TO LET PEOPLE IN

Because I want to stick to the basics, I'll share some simple ways that you can begin practicing vulnerability as well as assessing your vulnerability.

Share a Struggle

A simple way to begin practicing vulnerability is by sharing a struggle with the person you are trying to connect with. It could be as simple as sharing something that was difficult in your day, or as deep as revealing a personal struggle you're facing (financial, relational, health-wise, or other). Sharing something you're struggling with can be a powerful way to connect with someone because struggles are universal; they are something that all people can relate to.

Give a Compliment

We show our desire to take down the wall and connect when we can compliment and encourage the person we're communicating with. It reveals our desire to connect versus compete. It takes vulnerability to share how you feel about someone or what you admire about them, because you're taking the risk to go first when the compliment may not be returned or reciprocated. But that's not the reason you're doing it to begin with. Complimenting someone is being intentional to share how you feel in a way that spotlights the strengths of the person in front of you, instead of spotlighting your own.

Take Ownership

If you follow me online, have heard me speak, or have read any of my books, you know that ownership is basically my favorite word. Because we cannot change what we refuse to own. It requires vulnerability to take ownership and admit you did something wrong, or to confess that you could have done something better, because for most people it feels like you are choosing to reveal a deficit in yourself. But when you can take responsibility for something you did wrong or can own your role in a conflict or situation, you're practicing vulnerability because you are exposing the cracks in your wall rather than just trying to cover them up. Instead of seeing vulnerability as exposing a deficit, we should see it as an opportunity, an invitation to step into stronger, healthier, and more stable relationships. Ownership is the avenue to healing and change, because if you have no role in a situation, you also have no control in the situation. But when you claim a role in something, you also claim the right to change that situation. Ownership requires a level of vulnerability to take that first step and acknowledge an area in need of growth, strengthening, and transformation. But it paves the way for connection.

Express a Need

For some people, expressing a need is a really vulnerable action because ultimately, they don't trust people to meet their needs. Maybe they've asked in the past and been hurt, rejected, ignored, or let down, so they ignore, repress, or stuff their needs. They don't acknowledge their needs, and they certainly don't express their needs. But expressing your needs is one of the most powerful ways to build intimacy and connection. When you invite someone to meet a need, you are inviting them into intimacy and connection. You're revealing a void in your life and asking for help. This requires vulnerability because, ultimately, you don't know how that person will act or react to your request. But the more you can express your needs, and allow people to meet your needs, the more powerful your connections become.

Communicate a Hurt

It takes vulnerability to reveal when you've been hurt by someone because you have to show them a pain point inside of you and reveal a wound. It's easier to pretend you are fine and move on, but this repression starts to build the walls of self-protection around you even higher. When you can communicate a hurt, it invites the other person to meet you in that place and takes the relationship to new levels of trust and safety. Remember, communicating a hurt with vulnerability means the focus is on sharing your feelings of hurt rather than just telling the other person what they did wrong (that's not vulnerability; it's blame).

I don't know where you are with relationships right now, whether you're feeling really connected to the people around you or struggling with the feelings of distance and disconnect. But I do know this: vulnerability is the pathway to intimacy. Take inventory of where you may have put up the self-protective walls of polish and perfection and begin to build doorways of vulnerability instead.

VULNERABILITY IS THE PATHWAY TO INTIMACY.

TAKE OWNERSHIP

1. On a scale of zero to ten (zero being high walls of self-protection and ten being open doors), rate your current level of vulnerability with:

   - Family _____
   - Friends _____
   - Acquaintances _____

2. In which category of relationship above would you like to practice more vulnerability? Is there a specific person whom you would like to be more vulnerable with? Who and why?

3. Out of the five ways to practice vulnerability, which one do you struggle with the most? How can you take a step toward being more vulnerable in that way this coming week?

4. Why might you struggle with vulnerability? What are the experiences from the past that may have impacted your ability to be vulnerable and let down your walls?

13

DEALING WITH REJECTION

Thank You for That

I saw a meme that listed three ways to avoid rejection: 1. Say Nothing. 2. Do Nothing. 3. Be Nothing.

And I think that pretty much sums it up. Choose to interact with anyone in this world, and you will make yourself susceptible to the sting of rejection. It's part of the universal experience, and one that can't be avoided when it comes to interacting with people.

While I believe rejection is universally painful on many levels, I've also noticed that certain people respond far more strongly to rejection than others. Why is it that some people are so sensitive to it and go out of their way to avoid it at all costs, even if that means choosing isolation over interaction? I've worked with many people who have allowed the fear of rejection to be the motivating force behind why they do what they do.

I think of the young man who totally opted out of dating, even though he desperately wanted to be married someday, because he was afraid of being rejected by the women he was interested in. Or the young woman who desperately needed a job but refused to go on regular interviews because she was terrified she'd get turned down, which would magnify her insecurities. Or the married man who kept his needs to himself out of fear that if he asked too much of his wife, she would reject his requests for love. Or the woman who ended up blocking most of her friends and family out of fear that they would reject her, so she chose to preemptively reject them first. What is it about rejection that causes such a reaction in certain people?

WHY IT HURTS SO BADLY

I think the answer to that has to do with the pain points we carry underneath the surface of our lives. For many people, rejection hurts so badly because it's pushing on an emotional sore spot from our past. These are what I refer to as *triggers*: wounds from our past that get pressed upon in the present.[1] For many people, rejection is a trigger because it resurfaces older experiences of abandonment, betrayal, and hurt that have either been ignored, made light of, repressed, or avoided. Rejection triggers those deep hurts from the past that get activated in the present. And when you layer those two things together, you end up with an exponential amount of pain.

TRIGGERS: WOUNDS FROM OUR PAST THAT GET PRESSED UPON IN THE PRESENT.

The young man who had opted out of dating was also battling the pain of rejection by a mother who was very absent in his early childhood years.

The young woman who was avoiding job interviews was also battling the sting of peer rejection and severe bullying she had dealt with as a young girl.

The married man who kept his needs to himself was also battling the hurt of parents who were neither present nor available for him in his life.

The woman who rejected everyone before they rejected her was also battling the sting of the childhood trauma of growing up with a narcissistic and abusive father who consistently rejected her bids for love and affection.

IS IT ME OR YOU?

We're often told that rejection isn't really about us; it's about them. We're taught that the way to deal with the pain of rejection is to remind ourselves that the person rejecting us is the one who is really missing out by not choosing us. And while I believe those things are true, I also think we can learn a lot from our own personal response and reaction to rejection. The deeper the sting of rejection, the more likely it reflects a deeper wound in need of facing, acknowledging, and healing.

So, how can we deal with rejection whether it's superficial or substantial?

Identify Your Triggers

I encourage people to identify their triggers by looking for exaggerated emotional reactions to a situation. Sometimes, it's easier to identify the exaggerated response in hindsight, after the emotions have subsided. Have you ever looked back and wondered why you reacted so strongly to something? That's usually indicative of a trigger. If you find you struggle with a consistently strong reaction to rejection, it's time to take a step back and ask yourself why. Could there be other pain points below the surface that you've ignored? What experiences have you been through in the past that have reinforced the pain of rejection in your present? I always encourage my clients to map out their pain points by writing out a timeline of painful or hurtful experiences from the past, in chronological order. Specifically, look for the themes of rejection, abandonment, and feelings of being unwanted, undesired, or invalidated.

Part of identifying your triggers means looking back to see what experiences have made rejection so painful for you in the present. Pray over your timeline, asking God to help reveal to you the areas in your past that He wants to heal. Ask Him to give you a new perspective on those old stories. You can't change what happened in your past, but you can change your perspective on what happened. If you've identified a lot of past triggers, or you're having a hard time thinking of any at all, I encourage you to consider working with a counselor to help you unpack these things further and bring healing to some of these pain points in your life.

Shift Your Perspective

Not only is it important to begin shifting your perspective on the pain points of your past, but you have to be intentional about doing the same for the hurts in the present. I have always loved the phrase, "Rejection is God's protection," because I believe it's a perfect example of what it means to intentionally shift your perspective. The way you choose to tell yourself the story makes all the difference in your healing. You can either see rejection as evidence that there's something lacking in you, or you can see it as evidence of God's protection over you. There's a reason that job, relationship, situation, ministry, friendship, ____________________ (fill in the blank) didn't work out. A big part of that is God's sovereignty over your life, protecting you from the things you couldn't see, and then inviting you to pursue personal healing for yourself on a deeper level. How you tell yourself the story will either fuel your feelings of rejection or fuel your healing from rejection.

HOW YOU TELL YOURSELF THE STORY WILL EITHER FUEL YOUR FEELINGS OF REJECTION OR FUEL YOUR HEALING FROM REJECTION.

Adjust Your Measuring Stick

If our life revolves around the acceptance of others, it can feel like something inside of us has died when they reject us. When rejection hurts so badly, you have to ask yourself: What am I living for? When people become our measuring stick, the standard that determines our value and worth, then their rejection will certainly destroy us. There is a healthy level of people-pleasing in all of us, in that we want to love those around us and be loved by those around us. The problem happens when those people become our standard, our measuring stick, rather than God. This happens so subtly that sometimes we don't even notice we're going there until we feel the pain of rejection. It takes intentionality to continually stay aligned with the value and worth that comes from who we are in Christ: an unchanging, never-ending, unconditional value placed on us by a loving God. It may be easy to say it out loud, but harder to live it day in and day out. Yet when we can shift the posture of our heart to *that* measuring stick, we stop finding our value in what people think of us and start placing our value in what Jesus did for us.

I wonder what would happen if we could begin to see our rejection wounds as an invitation? An invitation to shift our perspective, dive into deeper healing of our triggers, and replace our unhealthy measuring sticks. If that's the case, then thank you for your rejection because it's inviting me into a deeper level of healing, perspective, intentionality, and growth, and for that, I will always be grateful.

TAKE OWNERSHIP

1. How painful does rejection feel to you on a scale of "not painful at all" (zero) to "very painful" (ten)?

2. If your answer ranged from seven to ten, have you been able to identify any pain points or triggers from the past that may make you more susceptible to the pain of rejection? What are some of those experiences?

3. Out of the three ways to deal with the pain of rejection (identify your triggers, shift your perspective, adjust your measuring stick), which area do you need to practice the most? How can you begin to take action?

4. Write about a recent rejection you experienced as well as how it offered you an invitation into deeper healing.

14

THE ART OF AN APOLOGY

#SorryNotSorry

I've been spending a lot of time on the topic of apologies lately. I'm not even exaggerating when I say there's got to be at least ten apologies happening daily in our home between the six of us family members (most of them involving three boys who shall remain unnamed). Some of you may know this fun fact, but we homeschool our kids, which means we all live together, eat together, do school together, and hang out together an extraordinary amount of time each day. In fact, at the writing of this chapter, due to some renovation projects in our actual house, all six of us are living together in a temporary townhouse with approximately 1,200 square feet, which gives us about 200 square feet per person if we're sticking to our zones. Which doesn't happen. Ever. Needless to say, we've been up in each other's space for a little while now, and we've got about three months to go. Which makes for a lot of opportunities for apologies, if you know what I mean.

But the most entertaining part about these apologies is watching how they unfold. I guess the perk of having four kids is that you literally have enough people to perform a social experiment every single day. And you can learn a lot about bad apologies by watching this social experiment. There's the *#sorrynotsorry* apology that comes with the least apologetic sounding voice possible. If you had your eyes closed and didn't know the language, you'd think you were hearing someone get called a rude name based on the tone and sound of the apology. Then there's the *least amount of effort possible to get this over with* apology, which literally uses the word *sorry* as the entire apology. The goal of this apology is to finish the conversation as fast as possible and take the least amount of ownership possible. As if one simple word has the power to undo all the hurt, words, and actions that preceded it. Don't forget the *backhanded apology* that sounds good at the start with the person taking some ownership for what they did and apologizing, only to go sideways when they add the words *but you* in the middle of it, and then proceed to tell the other person everything they did wrong or why they actually deserved what they got. This then nullifies the point of the apology altogether by making the conversation about the other person rather than the one who started the apology. Let's just say it has taken some serious work to teach the art of a good apology to these children (and by these children, I'm specifically referring to the above three little boys, who will remain unnamed...but you know who you are).

Being a parent of four kids is humbling on many levels, but I think the most humbling part is when you see glimpses of their childish behaviors mimicking the childlike behaviors that live inside of us as adults. I always say that there's a little child in each of us who tries to make his or her way to the surface of our lives, especially when we're feeling hurt. I can't say I've never been guilty of the #sorrynotsorry, least amount of effort possible, or backhanded apology. If we're honest with ourselves, we've all been there at some point. We're apologizing with our words, but not necessarily with our hearts.

WE'RE APOLOGIZING WITH OUR WORDS, BUT NOT NECESSARILY WITH OUR HEARTS.

Not only does that type of half-hearted apology prevent our relationships from recovering quickly, but it also prevents the recipient of the apology from being able to recover, process the apology, and begin to move forward. And not just in our emotional recovery, but in our physical recovery too. One study showed that people who received "pseudo apologies" had the same level of elevated blood pressure as those who had no apology at all after a conflict. Think about that for a moment. The half-hearted apology got the same physical reaction as no apology at all! It was only in those who received a genuine apology that researchers were able to see a rapid decrease in their blood pressure.[1]

There are times where you might genuinely believe you're giving a good apology, but the emotional or physical reaction you're seeing from the person in front of you says otherwise. Your words to a friend, your spouse, a relative, or someone else don't seem to be getting received the way that you intended. Here are some things to take into consideration about the way that you're apologizing.

PART 1: ACKNOWLEDGE WHAT IT IS YOU ARE SORRY FOR

A good apology starts by being specific. Using the basic phrase "I'm sorry" in and of itself doesn't work in an apology because it doesn't give context to what you're apologizing for. What you think you're apologizing for might be very different from what the other person needs an apology for. This is why it's important to be really clear when you're apologizing and acknowledge exactly what it is you're apologizing for: "I'm sorry I was distracted by my phone during dinner." "I'm sorry I had a rude tone with you." "I'm sorry I took out my frustration and stress from work on you." A healthy apology always starts with complete ownership and a specific acknowledgement. Be clear about what it is that *you did* that you are taking ownership of as your starting point. I clarify what *you did* because some people will try to sneak in the apology that sounds more like "I'm sorry you feel hurt" rather than "I'm sorry I hurt you." That's not ownership. So don't do it.

PART 2: VALIDATE THEIR FEELINGS

The next step to a healthy apology is to validate the feelings of the person you hurt. Try to put into words what they might be feeling and let them know you understand their perspective. Here's what it might sound like putting parts 1 and 2 together: "I'm sorry I didn't consider you when I made plans today. It made you feel hurt and unimportant to me." "I'm sorry I was distracted by my phone at dinner. You probably felt neglected and that you weren't my priority." It doesn't have to be long or elaborate, but the point is to validate the hurt as well as the feelings of the person you're apologizing to and show them you see their perspective.

PART 3: EXPLAIN WHAT YOU WILL DO DIFFERENTLY

A healthy apology doesn't just own what happened in the past; it owns what will change in the future as well. This reminds me of the time when Eli and Ella were five and seven years old, and Ella repeatedly asked Eli to stop spraying her with the hose outside. He didn't, and I eventually had to intervene. He gave as lovely of an apology as his little five-year-old self could muster, and then moments later, he sprayed her with the hose again. Call me crazy, but something about that gesture confirmed to me that he wasn't truly sorry. This part of the apology is so vital because it allows intentional thought to be put into what I'm going to do differently. A true apology doesn't just look at alleviating the pain point; it looks at changing the pattern. It answers the question: How can we do things differently moving forward? Putting all three parts together might sound like this: "I'm sorry I was distracted by my phone at dinner. You probably felt neglected and that you weren't my priority. From now on, I'll put my phone on the desk during dinner in order to give you my complete attention." We're all flawed human beings. A genuine apology doesn't mean we will *never* make that same mistake again (because most likely we will at some point), but it does show our intentionality to do things differently moving forward.

A TRUE APOLOGY DOESN'T JUST LOOK AT ALLEVIATING THE PAIN POINT; IT LOOKS AT CHANGING THE PATTERN.

PART 4: ASK FOR FORGIVENESS

This is the simplest part of a healthy apology, but in my opinion, it's also the most meaningful. It's asking for forgiveness. And it takes humility to do it in a way that really moves the apology from simple words coming out of my mouth to a posture of my heart. "Will you forgive me?" A few simple words have the power to convey your desire to reconcile, reconnect, and move forward together.

The next time you're confronted about something and need to apologize, don't let that little child inside of you come out and sabotage the interaction with a half-hearted apology. Ask God for humility, maturity, and the strength to apologize well, and then watch how a healthy apology leads to a healthy relationship. "Be completely humble and gentle; be patient, bearing with one another in love" (Ephesians 4:2).

TAKE OWNERSHIP

1. Of the pseudo apologies mentioned above, which one do you tend to be most susceptible to? What are some other ways you struggle with apologizing well?

2. Which of the four parts to a healthy apology do you tend to gloss over or fail to communicate when saying you're sorry?

3. When apologizing, do you tend to focus on alleviating the pain point or actually changing the pattern? How can you be more intentional with changing the patterns of conflict in your personal relationships?

4. Be aware of your tone, body language, and facial expressions during an apology. What are some ways you can be intentional to convey an apology with what you're saying as well as what your body language is conveying?

15

FORGIVENESS IS FOR YOU

Get Unstuck

I read that you're more likely to get a song stuck in your head if you end it halfway through rather than listening to it all the way to the end. And you may even be more likely to get a song stuck in your head that you don't like because you probably skipped it on your playlist while it was only part of the way through. Your brain is looking for closure. It's looking to finish the story. And when you interrupt the story prematurely, it's almost as though your brain gets stuck in a repetitive loop, looking for a way out.

As I was thinking about this concept, I thought about how it applies to other parts of life, in that some of the hardest situations to move past are the ones that seem to get interrupted in the middle of the story. The stories where we experience heartbreak, betrayal, loss, rejection, or abandonment at a time when we least expected it. I thought about how this concept of your brain getting stuck in a repetitive loop might apply to those situations as well. It seems like the places we get stuck the most are the stories that ended prematurely—the stories in which we never got the closure we had hoped for or expected. And so we find ways to loop that story over and over in our minds, obsessively ruminating about what should have been, could have been, or would have been different. If only.

SOME OF THE HARDEST SITUATIONS TO MOVE PAST ARE THE ONES THAT SEEM TO GET INTERRUPTED IN THE MIDDLE OF THE STORY.

Maybe that's why it was so hard for Bethany to move past that unexpected breakup, confused and heartbroken by the man she expected to marry.

Or why Mike is still struggling to make sense of the fact that his childhood best friend decided to step away from their friendship with no other explanation than, "It's just not serving me in this season."

Or why Lori still feels so stuck, four years after the blindsiding betrayal of a husband who left her and three little children for an unknown other woman.

Or why Ben continues to cycle through the events leading up to the loss of his job, getting let go after being betrayed by his board, who went behind his back and decided it was time to cut him loose rather than confronting him regarding their concerns or disagreements.

I think it's often the loose ends that are harder to deal with, because our brains and bodies just get stuck looking for closure, a way to tie up the story with a nice bow, or even just a basic knot, so that we can move forward and move on. But what happens in the stories where closure never comes? What happens when we never find out why, or understand the motive, or grasp the reasoning behind the hurt they caused us? What happens when it feels like closure is out of our reach? What happens when the story gets interrupted prematurely or unexpectedly?

CLOSE IT FOR YOURSELF

When I think about the word *forgiveness*, for me conceptually, it's synonymous with the word *closure*. It's the only way I've really been able to tangibly wrap my mind around the concept of forgiveness, and why it's so important for our personal healing and the healing of our relationships. Forgiveness is the closure we offer ourselves. It's the way we choose to end the story and tie up the loose ends. Forgiveness is how we finish the melody and get ourselves out of the trap of the constant loop of rumination and obsession. We get to decide how the story will end, and if someone hasn't offered us closure, we have the right, the ability, and the responsibility to choose closure for ourselves.

FORGIVENESS IS THE CLOSURE WE OFFER OURSELVES.

For Bethany, it means closing the door on her expectations of the future, ceasing to try to get answers that she'll never get, and choosing to build a new life here and now.

For Mike, it means closing the door on a childhood relationship, letting go of the pain of the past, and choosing to believe he has so much to offer the friendships that surround him today.

For Lori, it means closing the door on the marriage that once was, focusing on her own healing journey, and embracing her ability to create a beautiful life with the precious kids God has entrusted her with.

For Ben, it means closing the door on the ministry of his past, no longer dwelling on what should have been, and continuing to look ahead at what God is calling him to do in this new place with this new perspective and these new lessons.

If the door was left wide open, and a proper closure was never offered, we have the choice—no, we have the responsibility—to close that door ourselves.

FORGIVENESS IS FOR YOU

Forgiveness is the choice to tell ourselves the story from a different perspective. It's the choice to close a door that's been left wide open and finish the song that's been left unsung. It's choosing to move forward with intentionality and purpose, rather than allowing the pain and hurt to hold us back and keep us stuck. Because the tighter our grip on our hurt and pain, the more tethered we become to the person who hurt us. The more stuck we become in the place we were hurt. The more paralyzed we become by the way we were hurt.

THE TIGHTER OUR GRIP ON OUR HURT AND PAIN, THE MORE TETHERED WE BECOME TO THE PERSON WHO HURT US.

This is why, in teaching the concept of forgiveness, I think it's so important for people to understand that forgiveness is for you. It's your pathway out of a difficult and dark situation. It's the gift that God allows you to give yourself, choosing to let go of the person who caused the pain and allowing the pain to cause purpose. We choose to close the door ourselves by our intentionality in how we will act, interact, and react moving forward. You can't control what's been done to you, but you can always control how you respond to what's been done to you. You can't control what they choose to do, but you can control how you choose to react to what they do. Forgiveness is for you because it allows you to untether yourself from your pain and, instead, to rise above it by tethering yourself to God's purpose, believing with confidence that what man may have intended for evil, God still intends for good (Genesis 50:20). He redeems, He restores, and He doesn't waste a thing.

Is there a story that's been stuck on loop in your life due to a lack of closure? Is there a hurt that never came with a proper explanation or understanding? What part of your life might God be asking you to bring closure to by asking you to finish the song yourself? What part of your life might God be inviting you to enter into the gift of forgiveness, reminding you that forgiveness isn't actually for them. It's for you. For you to move forward. For you to get unstuck. And for you to be freed.

TAKE OWNERSHIP

1. Is there a conflict, hurt, betrayal, or other difficult situation that tends to play on repeat in your mind? What are the thoughts that often loop in your mind?

2. How can you bring closure to your situation in how you choose to finish the story?

3. "The tighter our grip on our hurt and pain, the more tethered we become to the person who hurt us." Consider that statement. Do you agree with the idea that forgiveness is for you? Why or why not?

4. Read these verses on forgiveness, in light of the fact that forgiveness is a gift to you: Matthew 6:12; Matthew 18:21-22; Mark 11:25; Ephesians 4:32; Colossians 3:13.

16

YOUR SOCIAL TEMPERATURE

On a Scale of Hot to Cold

On a scale of hot to cold, what would your social temperature be? I've always found it interesting how we often describe social interactions in terms of temperature. For example, someone might say that they have "warm feelings" toward someone while another person might talk about giving someone the "cold shoulder."

We tend to recognize and describe social patterns in terms of temperature. Not only that, many studies have shown that literal physical temperature also has an uncanny effect on our social temperatures. In fact, one carefully controlled Yale University study showed that people who had warmer hands (due to the fact that they were asked to hold a warm cup of coffee during the experiment) tended to have warmer ratings of the people they were interacting with than those who had cold hands.[1] It was almost as though their brain made the connection between the warmth of the physical to the warmth of the social.

When it comes to our social temperature, most of us would agree that socially warmer people are generally perceived as more likeable, kind, and interactive than colder people. But besides carrying a hot cup of coffee around all day long, how can we be aware of and control the social temperature we're exuding? What is it exactly that makes some people come across as warm and others come across as cold?

SOCIAL TEMPERATURE

It's a complicated conversation because someone can be extremely polite and well-mannered and yet still not be perceived as *warm*. I've interacted with many people who said all the right things yet came across as cool and distant and didn't exude that element of social warmth. So, I took to Instagram to get some opinions on what it is exactly that makes the difference between someone who comes across as warm versus someone who comes across as cold. Here's what the survey said are the things that help a person come across as socially warm:

- Smile!
- Eye contact is important.
- Ask good questions.
- Inviting demeanor.
- Welcoming body language.
- Tone of voice.
- Looking directly at the person you're talking to and not away.
- Good listening skills.
- Smile and eye contact!

- A smiling face with an open posture.
- Enthusiastic tone.
- Being engaged in the conversation.
- Active listening and demonstrating interest in the conversation.
- A wave.
- A hug or appropriate physical touch.

The list went on and on with *hundreds* of responses to this question, but it was interesting to note the categories that emerged (smiling and eye contact were the number one answer) that help us convey warmth in our social interactions. Here are the most significant ones.

Body Language

It's no surprise that we're back to the importance of body language (addressed in depth in chapter 6). The number one way people described social warmth (about 80 percent of responses) was through the use of intentional body language, specifically through smiling and eye contact (facial expressions). It's amazing how much your eye contact and your smile create the physical appearance of warmth before you even say one word. And science backs it up. A study on smiling showed that when people were exposed to photos of smiling versus non-smiling individuals, those with the smile were perceived as more likeable and evaluated more favorably than the non-smiling individuals. Not only that, but the smiling individuals were even perceived as more intelligent, and interestingly enough, created a "warm feeling" in the people who were viewing the photos.[2] We would all benefit from really analyzing the body language we exhibit, specifically our facial gestures, as they are the first thing people notice about us and the first indicator of our level of warmth.

IT'S AMAZING HOW MUCH YOUR EYE CONTACT AND YOUR SMILE CREATE THE PHYSICAL APPEARANCE OF WARMTH BEFORE YOU EVEN SAY ONE WORD.

Tone of Voice

You've heard it said that it's not what you say, but how you say it, that matters. Your tone of voice, as well as your ability to be intentional with your tone, has a significant impact on how you come across as well as the interpretation of your communication and interactions. One study even showed that what we hear (tone of voice) in communication may be even more significant than what we see (facial expressions) when it comes to interpreting the emotions of others.[3] In this particular study, participants were asked to watch two people interacting and analyze their emotions. Some watched in a well-lit room, while others watched in a dimly lit or pitch-black room. Participants who could only hear the interactions rated the emotions more accurately than those who could see the interactions, and even more accurately than those who could both see and hear the interactions. Our sense of hearing is very perceptive to the emotional environment that is happening around us. Our body is wired that way in order to keep us safe. But this same wiring also has a great impact on our perception of tone, especially in communication with others.

One thing to be aware of is that low tones always indicate more confidence, because your voice has a natural tendency to go to higher tones when you're nervous. In good public speaking etiquette, you're encouraged to speak in the lowest tone you feel comfortable speaking in (this is why most radio hosts tend to have lower-toned voices). Another thing to remember is that variety in your tone exudes more warmth than a monotone interaction. It's like listening to a song on the piano with a variety of notes rather than hearing someone play the same note over and over again. Limited variation in tone can sound robotic, which makes us feel disconnected and unattached to the speaker.

Volume is another aspect of our tone of voice to be used with intention. You don't want to be so quiet that people have to strain to hear you, or so loud that your voice is overwhelming, but a variety in your volume can be another way you indicate different emotions and exude warmth to the person you're communicating with. A louder volume can depict excitement to see someone, while a lower volume can depict caution or apathy. Have you ever thought about the importance of tone you exude when you're communicating? How you say something is just as important as what you're saying and can convey warmth, or lack thereof.

HOW YOU SAY SOMETHING IS JUST AS IMPORTANT AS WHAT YOU'RE SAYING.

Engaged Listening

The way you respond when someone is sharing can either signify a caring warmth or a cool apathy. Nodding your head and using vocal cues like "aaaah," "mmmm-hmmm," or "yeah" when someone is talking show that you are actively listening and convey agreement and reception of what's being said rather than apathy or distraction. The level to which you're engaged with the person speaking to you is one of the clearest ways to convey warmth (see more on this in chapter 10 on Listening Skills).

Physical Touch

In the Middle Eastern cultural background that I come from, it's totally normal, appropriate, and expected to greet people with welcoming physical touch, namely, in the form of a kiss on each cheek. In fact, choosing *not* to greet someone that way would come across rude, offensive, and distant. My cultural background gives context to 2 Corinthians 13:12, which encourages people to "greet one another with a holy kiss." And when you know someone *really* well or have *really* missed them, the number of kisses goes up! You will likely give or receive even more than two kisses. I still have a vivid memory of greeting a great aunt who had never met me before. She hugged me so tight and then gave me a total of ten kisses, five on each cheek, going back and forth to each cheek between kisses. Talk about a warm (but fairly long) welcome!

I'm not advocating for us to adopt this specific cultural norm (I'm almost laughing just imagining how that would go down in my home church in Lancaster, Pennsylvania, with a predominant culture having Dutch/German roots with a heavy Amish and Mennonite cultural influence). But I did find it fascinating, even within the framework of our Westernized perspective, how many people reported that physical touch was a specific way they felt warmth from someone. A firm handshake, a friendly hug, a pat on the shoulder, or a brief touch of the arm can be ways to convey warmth and connection. Appropriate touch conveys that you're not intimidated by, scared of, or avoidant of the person in front of you, but that you notice them and that you welcome them.

I was reading the story of Jesus healing the leper in the book of Mark, and I was struck by the way that Jesus showed warmth to a man who had been extremely ostracized and vehemently avoided by reaching out His hand and touching him. "Moved with compassion, Jesus reached out His hand and touched the man. 'I am willing,' He said. 'Be clean!'" (Mark 1:41 BSB). I don't know how Jesus touched him, but when I close my eyes to imagine it, I see Jesus taking His strong, gentle hands and compassionately embracing the man's face, looking him in the eyes, and telling him that He was willing to heal him. The thought of this interaction alone brings me to tears, as I imagine the compassion and warmth of Jesus, who reaches out His hands with intentionality and touches the ones whom others consider untouchable.

Appropriate physical touch can communicate kindness, friendliness, and warmth, but on the flip side, it can also be overdone and be misinterpreted, especially in the context of someone you don't know well or with someone of the opposite sex. Because on the other side of the spectrum, too much physical touch can come across as a lack of boundaries or even feel threatening. So be aware, and don't go overboard. Consider appropriate physical touch as a one-and-done thing during a conversation to convey warmth and welcome, and then leave it at that.

Social Energy

The energy and enthusiasm that you bring into an interaction has an effect on the level of warmth you exude. If you think about how you come across when you're tired, for example, versus when you're wide awake, the level of energy behind your interaction conveys your care, kindness, and prioritization of the conversation. (This is one of the reasons I've learned to avoid having important conversations with my husband after 11:00 p.m. One of us is a night owl, and the other isn't.) The level of social energy you bring to an interaction also communicates a level of warmth and enthusiasm. This may be easier for some than others (for example, extroverts versus introverts), but being aware of your energy and wielding it well can have a big impact on the warmth you exude.

Your level of warmth or lack thereof has a significant effect on the way you come across, as well as the way you're received and perceived by the people you're interacting with. This coming week, work on being observant and intentional with your body language, tone of voice, listening skills, physical interactions, and social energy. Warm up your social temperature and then watch how it impacts your relationships.

TAKE OWNERSHIP

1. On a scale of cool (zero) to warm (ten), what overall number would you rate yourself when it comes to your level of warmth in social interactions? _____

   What number would you rate yourself for first-time interactions with others? _____

   What number would you rate yourself in your friendships? ______

   What number would you rate yourself among your closest family and friends? _____

2. Which of the following areas do you need to pay attention to and be intentional with when it comes to portraying warmth: body language, tone of voice, engaged listening, physical touch, or social energy?

3. What was the level of warmth exuded in your family of origin growing up and in your cultural background? Rate it on a scale of cool (zero) to warm (ten). _____

4. How does this number compare to the overall number you gave yourself? Why do you think that might be?

17

WHAT'S THE RUB?

Assessing Your Triggers

Have you ever been triggered by someone?

You know what I'm talking about, right? Triggers are those moments we feel a strong, intense, or exaggerated emotional response to something that someone says or does. Take a moment to think about a time you were triggered in the last 30 days. Some of you might not even need 30 days, because you were triggered this morning! Sometimes we're triggered by things, but most often we're triggered by people. We're triggered in relationships.

It could be your boss, who just sets you off by the way he offers uninvited feedback or critique.

It could be your spouse, who frustrates you to no end when they ask questions that feel more like interrogations.

It could be the cashier at customer service, whose lack of basic manners makes your blood boil.

It could be that driver who cut you off on the way to work this morning, who brings out anger inside of you that you didn't know existed.

What is it about certain people and certain situations that brings out a reaction inside of us and rubs us the wrong way?

EMOTIONAL SORE SPOTS

Our culture tends to encourage us to run away from our triggers. We want to flee from anything that makes us uncomfortable or numb anything that feels even remotely painful. And we often do the same thing in relationships with people who rub us the wrong way or trigger us in some capacity. We want to distance ourselves from them or avoid them, and understandably so. But what if triggers are the very thing that invites us into the process of healing? What if triggers actually reveal what God wants to heal?

WHAT IF TRIGGERS ACTUALLY
REVEAL WHAT GOD WANTS TO HEAL?

I was leaving the house in a rush with my kids one day (it's basically an Olympic event trying to get four kids out of the house on time with everything they need and make sure nothing and no one gets left behind), when in my distraction, I slammed my shoulder on the coat rack on the way out. It *killed*. It was one of those pain levels where you instantly know it's going to leave a bruise. And it did. Later that day, underneath my sweater I noticed a large black and blue bruise on my shoulder. A little while later my husband came home and, as usual, leaned in to give me a kiss and put his arms around me. But without realizing it, he pressed up against the sore spot. "Ouch!" I winced and quickly pulled away from him. He didn't cause the sore spot, but he pushed up against it.

This right here is the exact thing that happens to many of us when we're triggered by someone. We may not have a physical sore spot, but we often have an emotional sore spot that was caused by something from the past. When we get close to others in relationships or in everyday socialization, people start rubbing up against us in our interactions. At some point, they will inevitably push up against our sore spots. They may not have caused the sore spot, but they press up against it, which causes a strong reaction inside of us, often a reaction that's disproportionate to the interaction. This explains why certain situations and even specific people rub us the wrong way and cause a strong reaction inside of us.

One of the most memorable moments in my training as a counselor happened during my time working on an adolescent psychiatric unit in a behavioral hospital. I was asked to do a mental health assessment for a recent admission, a teenage boy who had been brought in with symptoms of severe psychosis (meaning he was disconnected from reality, hearing and seeing things that weren't really there). Once he was settled in, I went into his hospital room with clipboard in hand and sat down in the chair across the room from him. I tried to make a little small talk and then began asking him some assessment questions as he stared blankly across the room at the adjacent wall and answered my questions with slow, one-word responses.

As a new counselor in my early twenties, I started feeling a little anxious by his demeanor. In my nervous energy, I grabbed the pearl earring I was wearing and twirled it around with my fingers while I talked to him. He glanced over at me, and suddenly everything changed. He instantly tensed up, got an angry look on his face, and without warning started to scream at me, "I hate you! You ruined my life!" Within seconds, he was making his way toward me in a complete rage, and I knew I needed to get out of that room fast. I got up and ran out of the room, all while quickly pushing my emergency pager, as he continued moving toward me at full speed. Within moments, a code was called and the security team was on the hospital floor. They worked to get him restrained while I ran for safety.

It was an intense moment, but looking back, it was also quite a lesson on this concept of triggers. You see, for many years, this young man had been abused by his mother. His hospital stay and his psychosis were a result of years and years of trauma that had never been dealt with. What I didn't know at the time is that his abusive mother also had a habit of twirling her earrings with her fingers. The moment he saw me doing that, he was triggered. My body language had triggered him in a way I couldn't have known. I may not have caused the emotional sore spot, but I had pushed up against it and caused a reaction inside of him.

You may not be triggered to that level, but I know there are things that set you off and people who rub you the wrong way. Instead of just making it about them (he's just bossy, she's just controlling, he's just rude), what about making it about you? Have you ever considered these triggers to be a learning opportunity, a chance for you to have insight and awareness of what you are feeling and why? An opportunity to take a look at what might be going on underneath the surface? An invitation to look inward, and examine the sore spots in your life that need healing?

I'm not saying we can heal every single one of our emotional sore spots completely until the glorious day we get to heaven. What I am saying is that the more often we're triggered, the higher likelihood that we have emotional sore spots in need of healing. But the more we heal our sore spots, the less likely we'll get triggered. Think of it this way: The fewer buttons you have, the less often people will be able to push your buttons! It's up to us to approach our triggers with curiosity and ask ourselves what God might be trying to reveal in our lives that He wants to heal. Triggers are a sign that there's more healing to be received.

Whoever said time heals all wounds didn't really understand trauma. Time doesn't heal all wounds; it doesn't have that kind of power. And some wounds, when left with time, will only get worse because they'll become more and more infected. But when we partner with God, acknowledge our wounds, and take the time to tend to our wounds, Jesus can begin to heal us.

So the next time you're feeling triggered, or someone really rubs you the wrong way, remind yourself of this: God reveals what He wants to heal. And then lean into the invitation of healing.

TRIGGERS ARE A SIGN THAT THERE'S MORE HEALING TO BE RECEIVED.

TAKE OWNERSHIP

1. Have you noticed a specific person or a pattern of people who tend to rub you the wrong way?

2. List out a few situations where you have been triggered in the past 30 days. Do you notice any patterns to those exaggerated emotional responses (for example: moments when you felt like you weren't good enough, felt disrespected, felt overlooked, or felt rejected).

3. How do you typically act and interact when you've been triggered?

4. What might be the underlying emotional sore spot for you, and where/when did it begin? What wound might God be revealing that He wants to heal?

18

PEOPLE PLEASING

What Served You Will Sabotage You

Every now and again I come across a phrase that stops me in my tracks. A few months ago, during our team meeting, one of the counselors on my team dropped a line that I find myself repeating on a regular basis: *Behind every people-pleaser was once a parent-pleaser.* If you consider yourself a people-pleaser, I wonder if you can also relate to this phrase. I know I can. As the first-born child in our family, I had an overarching sense of responsibility to the people around me. My belief was that it was my job to fill in the gaps where they needed to be filled and do my best to keep everyone happy. If you're a first-born, you can probably relate to that role. But even if you're not, there's a lot of truth in the idea that our people-pleasing tendencies run deep.

The reason this phrase holds true for so many people-pleasers is because we learn so much about relationships from how relationships were modeled to us in our formative years in childhood. The beliefs and roles that we develop in childhood, if left unchecked, are often the beliefs and roles that we carry into adulthood. I think of the child who grew up in a home where there was so much stress and chaos around them, whether from conflict, addiction, rebellion, or abuse, that the only way to keep the peace was to be the peace themselves: follow the rules, be a good listener, and make everyone happy. I think of the child who grew up in a home where everyone else around them seemed to have higher needs than they did so they learned to stuff their needs and silence their voice because, even in the most well-meaning family, it felt as though there was no space for them in that family dynamic. I think of the child who grew up with their value tied to their productivity or performance, with the underlying belief that to be smart or to be successful is to be loved. I think of the child who was raised in a religious atmosphere that taught them that they need to be good, righteous, perfect, or have it all together to be accepted by their parents, and ultimately to be accepted by God. Behind every people-pleaser was once a child who was trying to please. And now, those people-pleasing, performance-based tendencies have made their way into their day-to-day interactions.

BEHIND EVERY PEOPLE-PLEASER WAS ONCE A CHILD WHO WAS TRYING TO PLEASE.

This past year on my podcast, *Talk To Me*, I had two really memorable on-air sessions with two prominent women who struggled with people-pleasing in very different ways.[1] One of them was born into the world of Hollywood entertainment and performance, and as an actress of only five years old, had to learn really quickly how to act in such a way to please the producers on the other side of the audition and the audience on the other side of the screen. Her entire job hinged on people liking her. Pleasing others was part of her job, but in turn, it became a part of her life.

The other woman was born into a large and religiously conservative family, who from a very young age learned that she had to follow certain rules and behave in a specific way in order to have God's acceptance as well as the approval of others. Being good in order to please others equated to being loved, and in turn, became a part of her life.

Both women spent many years of their lives giving in to their internal struggle with pleasing people. And eventually, at different points in their lives, both women got to a place where their people-pleasing tendencies caused them to feel unworthy, inadequate, and unloved. They got to a point where the goal of pleasing people caused them to feel drained, depleted, and confused about their own identities. They both got to a point where their people-pleasing tendencies that served them in one season of life were now sabotaging them. Because it's really hard to try to please people and live in alignment with God at the same time.

SIGNS THAT YOU'RE A PEOPLE-PLEASER

Maybe you're not totally sure where you fall when it comes to people-pleasing. After all, we're called to care about and love the people around us. We're encouraged to consider the needs of others and serve those God has called us to serve. The problem comes when we do those things to please others rather than to please God. People-pleasing tendencies start to show up when we find ourselves interacting with others at the expense of our personal and spiritual well-being. You might struggle with people-pleasing if:

- You want to be liked by others, and their view of you impacts your view of yourself.
- You're often more in tune to what others might be thinking and feeling than you are with your own thoughts and feelings.

- You struggle to practice self-care and soul-care because you tend to put your needs last.
- You're a fixer and find yourself uncomfortable when others are feeling sad, hurt, or frustrated.
- You overapologize and feel guilty on a regular basis.
- You struggle to set boundaries because it feels like you're being mean or doing something wrong.
- You set high standards of perfection on yourself (and often feel like you're not measuring up), but you don't expect the same from others.
- You're not good at expressing your feelings and needs but grow resentful when others aren't in tune and continue to ask for more of you.
- You're motivated and reinforced by the affirmation and validation of others.
- You tend to feel secure in your identity when others are pleased with you or when they need you, but you question your identity when they are not pleased or do not need you.
- You weigh what others might think about you, or feel about you, as a big consideration in your decision-making process.

These are just some signals that indicate you might be a people-pleaser. But the question that follows is this: Is your tendency to please serving your life or sabotaging your life?

GOD > MAN

I don't think the solution to our people-pleasing tendencies is not to care about people and their opinions, but rather, to care about what

God thinks of us more. We can't set healthy boundaries, honor our capacity, and invest in our personal well-being if we're constantly trying to live up to the measuring stick of others. Jesus was such a good model of what it means to care more about what God thinks. He had a reputation of pleasing God more than pleasing man. In fact, people came to Him with their questions because they knew He wouldn't tell them whatever they wanted to hear just to please them, but that He would only tell them the truth: "Teacher, we know that you are true and do not care about anyone's opinion. For you are not swayed by appearances, but truly teach the way of God" (Mark 12:14 ESV).

WE CAN'T SET HEALTHY BOUNDARIES, HONOR OUR CAPACITY, AND INVEST IN OUR PERSONAL WELL-BEING IF WE'RE CONSTANTLY TRYING TO LIVE UP TO THE MEASURING STICK OF OTHERS.

His heart was set on pleasing God, and God alone. I love how the *Good News Translation* puts it in Proverbs 29:25, "It is dangerous to be concerned with what others think of you, but if you trust the LORD, you are safe." It is dangerous to be concerned with what others think of you because they cannot be your measuring stick. No human being, even at their best, will ever be able to give you an accurate measurement of your value or worth. When your goal is to make everyone happy, to be liked by all, and to be affirmed by those around you, you're no longer chasing after that which brings glory to God, but instead what brings glory to self. And you can't do both of those things at the same time. You must choose one or the other. And ultimately, one of those paths will end up guiding you toward God's calling on your life, while the other will end up keeping you away. Because if you're not careful, the same roles that served you in one season of life, if left unchecked, will sabotage you in another season. The solution is to ultimately believe that God's opinion of us is greater than man's opinion of us. And then begin to live that way.

TAKE OWNERSHIP

1. Out of the list of the 11 people-pleasing tendencies mentioned, how many can you relate to? ____ out of 11

2. Can you relate to this phrase: "Behind every people-pleaser was once a parent-pleaser"? Why or why not?

3. What were some of the people-pleasing patterns you had in your formative years? What is the underlying belief system that fuels your people-pleasing tendencies?

4. What are some ways you can begin caring more about what God thinks of you than what others think of you? What are some steps you can take to start changing the pattern?

19

SET THE TONE

Your Mood Is Contagious

Full disclosure: It's really hard for me not to judge some of the trends that end up going viral on Instagram. Like the #eggcrack challenge, for example, where someone thought it would be a good idea to pretend to bake with their child and then suddenly crack the egg on their head just to get their reaction on video, and then millions of other people decided to follow suit (all those kids are going to have future trust issues or get triggered every time they see an egg). Or what about the #pretendtohitbabyonthewall trend, where a parent would hold their toddler near a wall all while hitting their own hand on said wall loudly, to make the child think it was their head that got bumped (when it was really the parent's hand).

Despite how absurd these trends are, and even though I would never recommend any parent entertain themselves or others at the expense of their child, what I find most interesting about these trends is the fact that the children's reactions to these challenges were almost always a mirror image of the parent's reaction. If the parent acted overly concerned, rubbing the child's head and making them feel like they really did hit their head on the wall, the child would begin to cry. If the parent laughed and giggled and responded in a calm manner, the child would also laugh and giggle and remain calm. They took their cues of how to respond, not by assessing how they were actually feeling, but by absorbing the parent's emotional response.

Yet another viral Instagram video showed a mom who changed the atmosphere of her kitchen, which moments before included a crying baby in a highchair, by coming into the room singing and dancing to a good beat while using a pot with a wooden spoon as her makeshift drum set. Within moments, the child's sad mood lifted, and he was bouncing along to the positive beat, drumming on his highchair, and mimicking the mood and movements of his mom. He literally followed the beat his mom had set.

Child development theory explains that it's in human nature for children to look to others for cues on how they should respond emotionally. Not only that, but the cues they receive impact their emotional response. A child will mirror the emotions they see. This shows us the power of our mood, in that our emotional response to any given situation can literally change the atmosphere by causing both behavioral responses in those around us (for example, a child begins to cry in response to their parent's anxiety). It can also change physical responses in those around us (for example, a parent who is stressed can cause a cortisol spike in the observing child). The bottom line is this: We have a lot of influence in setting the tone and shifting the atmosphere around us. Our mood is contagious. And this doesn't just apply to the parent-child relationships; this applies to all of our interactions.

OUR MOOD IS CONTAGIOUS.

Back to those Instagram trends for a moment. The one my kids and I got a kick out of the most was watching the #fakescare trend, where one person suddenly acts terrified for no reason whatsoever and completely freaks out the person they are with. In the video, one person would pretend to see something scary and scream, yell, or jump away. And without even thinking about it, the person with them would have the exact same reaction. I watched a compilation of these trending videos with my kids recently and we all died laughing at the over-the-top reactions, until they started #fakescaring me, that is. Now it's not so funny.

EMOTIONAL CONTAGION

Imagine you had a really stressful day at work. You pull into your driveway, and you're fumbling around to find the keys to your house. Your stomach is growling with hunger, and you're feeling drained and exhausted. You step into your house and hear, "Surprise!" and within seconds you're surrounded by some of your closest family and friends, a table filled with food, birthday decorations all around, and the laughter and smiles of the people you love. I have a suspicion that would change your mood pretty quickly. Within moments, you'll find yourself matching the mood of what's going on around you, whether or not you're aware that it's happening. You'll be laughing with your friends as they talk about how surprised you looked, smiling as you greet each person there, and filled with happiness and joy no matter what happened at work leading up to that moment.

This phenomenon is called emotional contagion, and it's been researched more than ever in the last 20 years. The most significant thing about it is that so much of the emotional contagion is unconscious, meaning it happens without our awareness. You're more likely to smile when you walk into a room full of happy people at a surprise party, just as much as you're likely to frown and feel somber when you're walking into a funeral. Research shows that you will begin to mirror the emotions around you. The important thing about emotional contagion is that it can happen with both positive and negative moods. Science often refers to the concept of mirror neurons, discovered by psychologist Elaine Hatfield, to describe this phenomenon taking place in our body where certain neurons fire inside of our brain that mimic the neurons being fired in the brain of the person in front of us. For example, research shows that people are more likely to imitate or mirror the body language of the person in front of them.[1] This explains why you're more likely to yawn when you see someone yawning in front of you. Not only that, but you will likely find yourself smiling when someone else smiles at you, because your body is compelled to mirror the mood in front of you whether you intend to do so or not.[2]

In workplace settings, a fascinating study showed that the emotional contagion of the feeling and mood of anger had a very high effect on the workers and led to more cognitive failures and errors throughout the entire team.[3] Your mood is contagious and being aware of this concept is important for two reasons: 1. It brings your attention to how influential you are in setting the mood of the atmosphere around you, and 2. It reminds you that you are susceptible to the mood and emotions of others, so that you're less vulnerable to shifting into a negative space. Because we are both influential and susceptible, we need to make it a high priority to take ownership of our own mood.

In counseling, we call this self-regulating. In order to be able to shift the mood in others, you first have to learn how to set the mood in yourself. Being in tune and aware of how you feel, and responding to those emotions in healthy ways is foundational to your ability to set the mood and have influence in your day-to-day interactions.[4] Your ability to be aware of your own emotions makes or breaks your ability to influence the environment around you. In working with thousands of people, I know that most people aren't actually in tune to their feelings throughout the day. They lack insight and awareness, or don't take the time to stop and look inward. You can be carrying an edge of frustration, anger, irritation, apathy, annoyance, inadequacy, insecurity, hurt, overwhelm, or stress (just to name a few) to your mood without even realizing it. It begins to impact the people around you. And if you're lacking in awareness, sometimes they can feel it even before you can. Influence always starts with awareness.

INFLUENCE ALWAYS STARTS WITH AWARENESS.

So let me ask you this: What is the atmosphere you have set today? If people were consistently mirroring your mood, how would that change the atmosphere around you for the good or for the not so good? When you walk into a room, how does your mood shift the environment? Are you aware of your own feelings and willing to take ownership of your influence? Your mood is contagious, so be careful with it.

TAKE OWNERSHIP

1. Have you noticed emotional contagion in your life, whether regarding your influence on others or their influence on you? Where or in what relationships do you see this play out most often? How can you alter your own mood and/or set boundaries to be less susceptible to the negative moods around you?

2. Have you taken inventory of your emotions and mood today? If so, write out what you are feeling and why.

   If not, take five minutes to do so by following the promptings below.

   - Close your eyes and take three deep breaths: breathe in for five seconds and release for ten seconds.
   - With your eyes closed, scan your body from the top of your head to the bottom of your toes, bringing awareness to each section, to see if you are carrying physical tension anywhere.
   - With eyes still closed, review the events from the day in your imagination, specifically noting any moderate to strong emotions you felt (stress on your way to work, frustration at the meeting, overwhelm with the kids).

- With eyes still closed, review the events from the past week, specifically noting any moderate to strong emotions you felt.
- What emotions are you carrying in this moment or in the moments surrounding this moment? Put a few words to what you might be feeling. If you need some help identifying feelings, go to DebraFileta.com/resources to access a free chart with a list of over 500 emotions.

3. In what ways have you influenced the atmosphere today? How will you choose to set the mood moving forward?

20

PRACTICE HUMOR

Not Everyone Is a Comedian

I've had a lot of conversations with my kids over the years, from serious to silly to spiritual and everything in between. I often wish I had a little notebook in my back pocket so I could write down all the details of the conversations I want to remember. Sometimes, I get out my phone and jot down a meaningful interaction in my notes app to try to keep that moment in my memory. Because realistically, if they don't get written down, most of those moments end up fading in the millions of words and memories I've exchanged over the years between all four of them. Yet there are some conversations that will be seared in my mind *forever*. I never even had to write them down. And most of them are the funny ones! Let me share a few of my favorite hilarious conversations with my kids:

• • •

I was doing a math problem with Eli when he was in second grade that read something like this: "Mrs. Smith was hosting a dinner party. She needed 32 skewers for chicken and 56 skewers for beef. How many skewers did Mrs. Smith need?" To which Eli replied in all seriousness: "I have a question." "Yes, Eli?" I responded. "What time's the party?" Apparently, he was less concerned about math and more concerned about getting to that party and eating those skewers!

• • •

After finishing up reading the story of Joseph from the Bible and processing with the kids, I asked: "What is the lesson we get from today's story?" Five-year-old Ella replied: "If your brother annoys you, throw him in a pit!" Needless to say, we had to review that lesson a few more times.

• • •

At age eight, Ezzy overheard us talking about a singles conference where I was speaking out of town. Trying to convince us to let him and his siblings come along on the trip, he said, "We can come! We're single!"

• • •

Getting ready for church one Sunday morning, Ethan (age four) said to me, "Mom, I love big church!" (Big church is what he calls the service for the adults.) "Oh, that's great, Ethan! What do you love about big church?" I asked. "They give you snacks!" he replied enthusiastically. "What snacks?" I asked, racking my brain to understand what he could be referring to. Without missing a beat he replied, "Bread and juice!" Apparently, we have some work to do in the theology department.

• • •

DRAWN TO HUMOR

It's amazing how most of the things that really stick in your mind are the funny moments. I bet you could think of a few funny moments from your life if you took the time. Humor is memorable and meaningful to us as human beings. It brings joy to the heart and lightness to the spirit. Laughter is indeed a gift (Psalm 126:2). People are drawn to humor. So much so, that studies show that 91 percent of men and 80 percent of women report that a sense of humor is the number one quality they want in a life partner.[1] There's a psychological reason for that. When we're exposed to something humorous that makes us laugh, a series of triggers happens in our mind that ultimately leads to the release of the neurochemical dopamine, the feel-good chemical in our body. And just like any dopamine-releasing activity, our body wants more of that pleasurable feeling, and so we're naturally drawn to its source. In short, humor attracts the attention of others because it physiologically makes them feel good, and people like to feel good. Not only that, but because humor usually comes with an element of surprise (because it's typically unexpected), it reinforces our brain's reward system, keeping us interested and engaged, waiting for another fix of humor.

Humor cultivates an environment where people feel more connected than they would otherwise feel because the dopamine release calms the body, increases all the good feelings, and in turn, decreases the stress. It's like a pressure release valve. When this happens in a group setting, the people who are laughing together feel more connected and closer to each other. This is why many public speakers, and even pastors, try to incorporate an element of humor in their messages, to draw in their audience with a dopamine boost.

HUMOR CULTIVATES AN ENVIRONMENT WHERE PEOPLE FEEL MORE CONNECTED THAN THEY WOULD OTHERWISE FEEL.

But before you start cracking jokes in social settings, it's important to realize that not all humor is created equally. Researchers categorized humor into four categories: Self-enhancing humor (humor that enhances others' perception of you), affiliative humor (humor that enhances your relationship with others), aggressive humor (humor that enhances yourself at the expense of others), and self-defeating or self-deprecating humor (humor that decreases others' perception of you). As you can probably guess, self-enhancing and affiliative humor were received more favorably than aggressive and self-defeating humor.[2] People want humor that makes them feel good, not the opposite effect! I've been around far too many people whose version of humor ends up putting themselves down or putting down those around them. That type of humor puts people in self-protective mode, causing them to be on guard and to feel disconnected.

CAN YOU LEARN TO BE FUNNY?

We all know people who seem to be naturally funny. But is humor something that you're born with or something you have to learn how to use? Overall, there seems to be an underlying genetic component linked to an increased sense of humor, particularly smiling and laughing.[3] But just like any behavioral trait, there's always a combination of nature and nurture. If you're someone who doesn't consider yourself a funny person, is humor something you can train yourself in? I say yes. On a scale of serious to silly, I definitely lean toward serious. But over the years, I've both cultivated and embraced my humor and allowed it to shine through more in my writing, speaking, and my everyday life. Fast forward to today: I actually think I'm hilarious (okay, maybe that's a stretch). But ultimately, humor has truly been a gift and added so much joy and laughter to our lives. And that is something I believe we don't take seriously enough. Scripture reminds us that there is a time to weep and a time to laugh (Ecclesiastes 3:4).

I often wonder if we don't spend enough time on either side of that spectrum. Maybe we're afraid to feel too deeply, so we stay in the safe middle ground, neither feeling too much sadness nor allowing ourselves to feel too much joy.

You don't have to be a comedian, but just like any muscle, humor is something I believe we can train ourselves to grow in for the purpose of making the most of life, connecting with people in a deeper way, intentionally cultivating an environment of joy, leaning into the gift of laughter, and tearing down the walls of awkwardness and discomfort. "This is the day that the LORD has made; let us rejoice and be glad in it" (Psalm 118:24 ESV). It's a gift to share joy and laughter. So if I were you, I'd start by googling *how to be funny* and get a little practice in this coming week. Best case scenario, you'll make someone else laugh. Worst case scenario, you'll make yourself laugh. And either one of those outcomes slowly moves our people skills in the right direction.

MAYBE WE'RE AFRAID TO FEEL TOO DEEPLY, SO WE STAY IN THE SAFE MIDDLE GROUND, NEITHER FEELING TOO MUCH SADNESS NOR ALLOWING OURSELVES TO FEEL TOO MUCH JOY.

TAKE OWNERSHIP

1. On a scale of serious (zero) to silly (ten), what number would you give your sense of humor if ten is the funniest? _____
2. What role did humor play in your childhood or family of origin?
3. How can you intentionally use humor and laughter this week to build an environment of connection and foster more joy in your life?
4. Take a moment to recall a funny memory you have and thank God for the gift of laughter.

21

WE ALL HAVE A LITTLE NARCISSUS IN US

Pride Repels

I already told you about one of my top three pet peeves earlier in this book (do you remember it? Here's a hint: Don't interrupt.). You want to hear another one? It's when people use diagnostic terms in the wrong way. And at the top of the list is a little word that has been thrown around a lot over the past couple years: *narcissist*. I can't tell you how many times I've heard someone call someone else a narcissist or label them with NPD (narcissistic personality disorder). I've seen countless social media posts and reels describing someone as a narcissist without an official diagnosis (likely without fully understanding the complexity of the term). It's a word that's become more popular with time, and even a part of everyday lingo.

In case you don't know the background for this term, let me tell you the story from which it originates. There's a story from Greek mythology about a fictional character named Narcissus. He was so incredibly handsome and good-looking that people began to fall in love with him. But instead of receiving their love, in his pride and arrogance, he looked down on them in disdain. He believed he was too good for anyone and everyone. One day, Narcissus went to a pool of water to get a drink. While he was there, he looked down at his own reflection and fell in love with the handsome face looking back at him. The story goes that he became so infatuated with his own image that he couldn't leave and eventually died there alone by himself.

The story of this mythical creature is what has shaped our meaning and understanding of the term *narcissist*. In fact, the DSM-5-TR (*The Diagnostic and Statistical Manual* for counselors) describes narcissistic personality disorder, diagnosed in less than 6 percent of the population, with 50 to 75 percent of those who receive the diagnosis being men (no offense, guys, I'm just quoting the stats), as a mental health disorder with a preoccupation of self. Here are some of the defining characteristics of this diagnosis:

- Exaggerated self-appraisal
- Sees oneself as exceptional
- Sense of entitlement
- Lack of empathy
- Impaired ability to recognize the feelings and needs of others
- Limited interest in others' experiences
- Self-centeredness
- Belief that one is better than others
- Condescending toward others
- Admiration seeking[1]

I don't know about you, but if we're honest with ourselves, I think we'd all see a little bit of ourselves in that list. Whether or not we'll admit it, and whether or not we've reached the extreme, there's a little bit of Narcissus in each one of us. Moments when we believe we're better than the rest. Moments when we're seeking admiration and applause. Moments when we're unable or unwilling to see someone else's perspective. Moments when we're more interested in our own needs than the needs of those around us. Moments of self-centeredness and self-absorption. There's a little bit of Narcissus in each one of us, and his nickname is *Pride*.

PRIDE REPELS

I think one of the very first things that's revealed in our relationships is our tendency toward pride. And if we're not careful to identify it and deal with it, we'll find that it's the beginning of the end of our relationships, because "pride goes before destruction, and a haughty spirit before a fall" (Proverbs 16:18 ESV). Pride will always keep people away, because there's no room for them or their perspectives in the equation. It repels us from relationships because we choose self over others. It keeps us in isolation and loneliness because in choosing self and self alone, we push others away, and just like Narcissus, we end up alone with ourselves.

PRIDE WILL ALWAYS KEEP PEOPLE AWAY, BECAUSE THERE'S NO ROOM FOR THEM OR THEIR PERSPECTIVES IN THE EQUATION.

The thing about pride is that often it's so subtle that we don't notice it. It begins to take root and grow, slowly creeping into our lives until it chokes out our relationships. It affects our ability to feel a positive emotional connection to the people around us (*Look at all their flaws!*), it gets in the way of our empathy and desire to see another person's perspective (*They are the problem!*), and even more concerning, it distorts our ability to see our own role and where we've been wrong (*This isn't my fault!*). I would go as far as to say that pride is the number one thing that negatively impacts our relationships and interactions and causes conflict and tension because "where there is strife, there is pride" (Proverbs 13:10). Problems and pride. The two will always go hand in hand.

The most dangerous thing about pride is that it blinds us from our own flaws and prevents us from taking ownership of the things we need to adjust and change. It puts the impetus of change on the other person, leaving us with no role in the equation. But like I always tell my clients, and often remind myself, "If you have no role, you also have no control." If we really want to make an impact in our relationships, we need to understand our role and responsibility in every interaction.

Have you ever been in a rush to get out the door and there's something you're looking for that you can't seem to find? Maybe it's your keys or glasses, your wallet or your shoe (yep, that last one happens in our house more often than I'd like to admit). I tend to be an organized person, but with four kids, life can get a little disorganized. I find myself running around the house like a crazy person, looking for that lost item in the most obscure places. And do you know what's even more annoying than realizing you're missing something one minute before you walk out the door? Finding it later in the most *obvious* place. Sometimes, I even find it in the place where I looked before, but I didn't have the eyes to see it the first time around because I was flustered with the emotional rush of trying to get out of the house. We often miss things that are right in front of our eyes because we're blind to them in the moment of heightened emotion.

It's so easy to do this with our *things*, and even easier to do this with *ourselves*. In the heat of an argument or disagreement or in the middle of a conflict, we can be so quick to see the flaws of others, and so slow to see our own. If we're not aware, we'll see what we want to see instead of what's really there.

And pride is the biggest blinder of all. This is why in the book of Matthew, Jesus tells us that if we really want to make a shift in our relationships, we need to first look at our own role in the interaction. He says,

> Why do you look at the speck of sawdust in your brother's eye and pay no attention to the plank in your own eye? How can you say to your brother, "Let me take the speck out of your eye," when all the time there is a plank in your own eye? You hypocrite, first take the plank out of your own eye, and then you will see clearly to remove the speck from your brother's eye (Matthew 7:3-5).

What I appreciate about this verse is that it starts with us. It starts with taking a role and responsibility in every interaction. If you want to do relationships well, if you want to master your people skills, if you want to make the most of your interactions and allow them to be the healthiest they can be: *First* take the plank out of your own eye. It's step one. It's the place where we have the biggest role to play and the most power in making a change. It's a serious call to let go of the false idea of who we think we are and open our eyes to the reality of who we really are—flawed human beings; sinners in need of grace; and people with a tendency to make mistakes.

PRIDE IS THE BIGGEST BLINDER OF ALL.

That's not to say that we don't offer feedback, critique, advice, or suggestions to others. It's also not to say that we don't share our feelings and how we've been hurt with those who hurt us. But according to Matthew 7, that is the *second* step. First remove the plank from your own eye, and then you will see clearly to remove the speck from your brother's eye. We have to be able to "see clearly" in order to accurately assess what's going on in front of us and be able to communicate that clearly.

Ask yourself this: When it comes to your people skills, how do you tend to respond when there's a conflict, argument, disagreement, or difference in opinion? Are you quick to look at the plank in your eye, or do you rush to adjust the speck in your brother's? Do you consider the feelings, thoughts, and opinions of others, or is your primary goal to communicate your own? We all have a little Narcissus in us, and it's that very same tendency that will lead us quickly down the road to isolation, emotional distance, and separation from others. For our relationships to have any hope, we have to let go of our pride in exchange for something greater—humility.

TAKE OWNERSHIP

1. There's a little bit of Narcissus in each of us. Look through the traits of NPD in this chapter. Which tendencies do you see in yourself the most?

2. Consider the idea that pride repels relationships. In what ways has pride impacted the relationships in your personal or professional life?

3. How do you tend to respond when there's a conflict, argument, disagreement, or difference in opinion? Are you quick to look at the plank in your eye, or do you rush to adjust the speck in your brother's?

4. Take some time to pinpoint specific examples of where and when you've been prideful. Spend some time in prayer and confession and ask God to help give you a heart of humility in your relationships.

22

THE H WORD

Humility Attracts

What's your reaction to the word *humility*? Think about that for a moment.

I've noticed the word in and of itself brings about different reactions in different people. Many people have grown up seeing the word humility through a negative filter, and equate it to weakness, insecurity, or passivity. Others see humility as a spiritual challenge, a call to have a proper understanding that we are *nothing* and God is *everything*. Others still see humility as the act of passing the credit along to God, rather than taking credit for ourselves, like when Philadelphia Eagles coach Nick Sirianni started his post-win speech by giving God the glory for their 2025 Super Bowl win (Go Birds!).[1]

But what if I told you that humility isn't a behavior or even a feeling, but it's rooted in an underlying belief system that forms how we feel toward others as well as how we act around them? Humility is a perspective. It's grounded in the ultimate truth that all human beings are innately valuable, intricately created, and intentionally made in the image of God (Psalm 139:14; Genesis 1:27). If you really, truly, grasp that information, it changes how you interact with others, as well as how you feel about yourself. You can't help but love others well when you're perceptively in tune to their innate value and worth. When people are valuable because they are valued by God, they become valuable to the people of God as well. When people are precious to you because they are precious to God, it changes everything (Isaiah 43:4).

Who is the most famous person you've ever met or had some sort of interaction with? What did interacting with that person feel like? On a recent trip down to Florida, we passed by an affluent neighborhood where celebrities like Michael Jordan, Celine Deon, and a few other notable names were said to live. Soon after that, we passed by the school where it was said that some of these celebrities' children attended. The driver of the car pointed in that direction and then said something like, "Imagine how cool it would be to go to school with MJ's kid!" I mean, that would be pretty cool. But why? It's because of the value and worth placed on that child by way of the fame of his dad. When someone is perceived to be valuable, it increases our desire to be near them, to interact with them, and to get to know them.

Now imagine we viewed everyone we met through that lens. Imagine we saw everyone by the value and fame and worth and status passed down to them by their Father, their Heavenly Father. God Almighty. Jehovah Jireh. The Great I AM. The King of kings and the Lord of lords. I don't know about you, but having that perspective front and center would drastically change how I interact with the people in my everyday life: from my husband, to my kids, all the way to the cashier at Target. A proper belief system doesn't elevate people *above* ourselves (because we're *all* made in the image of God), but it should elevate the value and worth we perceive in them. It should elevate our perspective of them. And it should definitely elevate our love for them.

WHAT GETS IN THE WAY

What if I told you that higher levels of humility are correlated with higher levels of commitment, trust, forgiveness, and an overall increase in relationship satisfaction? If pride repels relationships, then the opposite of that is also true, and it's also scientifically true. Humility attracts. It brings people close. It invites people in. It creates an environment of trust. But if it's that easy, why is humility so difficult to practice? I believe it has something to do with our self-protecting, self-preserving, and self-promoting tendencies.

Put it this way: We're wired to keep ourselves safe. Our brain and body neurologically work together to protect us from perceived danger. If you see a car coming toward you at 75 miles per hour, you'll run. If you touch something hot, you'll quickly move your hand away. If you hear a loud noise, you'll react. Your sympathetic nervous system kicks into action, and your fight-or-flight response takes over, putting you on high alert and ready for action.

Now, pair that natural response system with life experiences where we've been hurt by some and neglected by others. Situations in life when we weren't protected, cared for, loved, valued, or taken care of the way we ought to have been. Those difficult relational situations heighten our desire for self-protection, self-preservation, and self-promotion even more. And not only that, those types of situations increase our distrust in the people around us. We become more inclined to think of ourselves as a protective mechanism. *I have to protect my own value* becomes our underlying belief system, rather than *I have to protect their value.* It's impossible to be humble when our primary goal is self-preservation, self-protection, and self promotion. It's hard to consider others in a genuine and authentic way when we're ultimately after the goal of caring for ourselves.

That's not to say we don't care for ourselves by setting boundaries, choosing safe relationships, and being in tune with our environment

(I talk more about the importance of this healthy balance in my book *Soul Care*), but when our underlying belief system is trapped in self-preservation mode, we don't even have the mental or relational capacity to consider others. Because you can be humble only to the level at which you trust God to protect, preserve, and promote you. "Humble yourselves before the Lord, and he will lift you up" (James 4:10).

YOU CAN BE HUMBLE ONLY TO THE LEVEL AT WHICH YOU TRUST GOD TO PROTECT, PRESERVE, AND PROMOTE YOU.

Humility is an entirely new way of believing and living. It's a radical belief system that asks us to consider the *why* behind how we treat people. It shifts our perspective from *me* to *God*. God is my protector, my provider, and my promoter. The more I can receive that from Him, the freer I am to function in humility in every interaction.

- "For all those who exalt themselves will be humbled, and those who humble themselves will be exalted" (Luke 14:11).
- "[He] shows favor to the humble" (Proverbs 3:34).
- "Humility comes before honor" (Proverbs 15:33).
- "He crowns the humble with victory" (Psalm 149:4).

Humility is not a weakness; it's a strength. It's the only way to function in the economy of God's kingdom that flips everything on its head. If you want to be protected, preserved, and promoted, you can only get there by way of humility, following in the ultimate example of our God who humbled Himself to the point of death, and then was raised to life and exalted to the highest place above every name (Philippians 2:8-9). "If we will take care of humbling ourselves, we can trust God to take care of exalting us."[2] Humility can only come from a place of confidence—confidence in God.

I think it's safe to say that humility is our greatest people skill. It's the superpower by which we accurately perceive God, self, and others. It's the underlying belief system that changes how we feel about others and, in turn, how we act toward them. When you're struggling to be humble in a certain place or with a specific person, dig a little deeper and get to the root of your *why*. God honors the humble. He raises them up. And He trusts them with more. If you're struggling in relationships today, start by assessing this important area of your life. Because humility will always attract.

HUMILITY IS OUR GREATEST PEOPLE SKILL.

TAKE OWNERSHIP

1. What is your initial response to the word *humility*? Do you tend to see it as a strength or a weakness? Do you correlate humility with insecurity or confidence? Why or why not?

2. When it comes to feelings of self-protection, self-preservation, or self-promotion, which of those three areas do you struggle with the most? Why? What are some past experiences or relationship wounds that may have contributed to this?

3. Think about your reaction to this phrase from the chapter: *You can be humble only to the level at which you trust God to protect, preserve, and promote you* (page 170). Do you agree or disagree, and why or why not?

4. In what specific places and with which specific people do you need to practice humility?

23

SOCIAL ANXIETY

One Perspective Shift That Changes Everything

"Do you get nervous before you speak?" Someone asked me this at an event recently right before I went on stage to speak to a group of almost 1,000 people. I had to think about that question for a moment because the answer to that has drastically changed over the years.

When I first got dropped into the world of speaking a decade ago (and I say *dropped* into the world of speaking because I literally went from very minimal public speaking and mainly one-on-one interactions in my counseling office to being asked to be the keynote speaker at a conference at Saddleback Church, one of the largest churches in America, in just a few months' time), I was really anxious. I used to describe public speaking as the emotional equivalent of climbing up Mount Everest. (Okay, maybe not Everest; that's a little extreme, but at least a mountain with a 10,000-foot elevation. How about something in Colorado?) It felt like an emotionally draining exercise. And it wasn't just the speaking itself that was emotionally draining; it was everything leading up to it. The entire week before I spoke, I would feel the strain of the emotional toll of having to teach in front of 100;

500; 1,000; 3,000; or however many people I had to speak in front of. And the bigger the audience, the more anxiety I felt.

I didn't want to feel anxious; in fact, I hated the feeling. I knew without a shadow of a doubt that I was walking in what God had called me to do, yet I despised the emotional toll of the anxiety that I carried up until I spoke. It felt like a heavy burden. I'd be flooded with thoughts about what I was presenting, how it would be received, how I would communicate, what people might think and feel, and whether or not I could keep their attention. I knew in my heart that I had something really important to say, a message that I believed God had given me, but I wondered if I would be able to communicate it effectively. I wonder if that's what Moses felt when God asked him to go speak to Pharoah, and he started listing out all the reasons why he might not be able to do what God had called him to do: *I'm not eloquent enough, I'm slow in speech, I've never been a good communicator* (Exodus 4). Social anxiety is guaranteed to creep in when we start to list out all that we lack. The more I focused on myself, what I did or didn't have, and my own abilities, the more anxious I would feel.

SOCIAL ANXIETY IS GUARANTEED TO CREEP IN WHEN WE START TO LIST OUT ALL THAT WE LACK.

Maybe you're not a public speaker. Maybe you've never been asked to lead a large group of people or deliver a message in a social setting, but this concept of social anxiety plagues so many people in small ways and in big ways. Think of it this way: How do you feel when you walk into a room of people you don't know very well? How do you feel when you're asked to answer questions or offer feedback in a group setting? How comfortable are you when you're interacting with strangers in a large group setting, or how about a small group setting?

I remember working with a young adult woman in my counseling office who felt so much social anxiety she couldn't even order food at a drive-through because she was so paralyzed by feelings of anxiety whenever she had to interact with someone she wasn't familiar with. I think of another gentleman whose social anxiety was so high that he became addicted to drugs just to cope with the intense isolation. He was paralyzed by his fear to the point where he struggled to interact in everyday relationships. Even coming to counseling to talk to me took a huge emotional toll on him, and he was only there because his parents threatened to kick him out of the house if he didn't come. I think of another woman who would get so flustered at her work meetings, and she dreaded those days to the point of feeling sick to her stomach on the day of a meeting. Her face and neck would get so red if she was called on to speak or answer a question, and she would feel like she was just about to melt into a puddle in her chair.

Social anxiety is a significant problem for many people, and while there are different levels of struggle and different reasons why we struggle and different treatment methods depending on the severity of the struggle, there are some baseline underlying beliefs and thought patterns that tend to either perpetuate the anxiety or keep it under control.[1]

THE THOUGHT THAT SHIFTED EVERYTHING

I was preparing to head out of town for a rather large speaking engagement, and I was in my office looking over my notes, printing out some papers, and thinking through what I needed to prepare when I had an intrusive thought that interrupted my internal dialogue: *You are going to give, not to receive.* I stopped in my tracks and replayed that thought in my mind a few times. I thought about Jesus's words recorded in the book of Acts: "It is more blessed to give than to receive" (Acts 20:35), and then I processed what it meant to me in this specific setting. *I am going to give, to serve, to offer the gift I've been given. I am going to communicate a message God has given me. This is not about me; this is about Him. Therefore, the pressure is not on me; it's on Him.* I kid you not when I say that, just like that, in that literal moment, my underlying anxiety decreased by 80 percent. I felt so much lighter, so much freer, and so much less anxious.

The one thought that shifted everything for me is to own the fact that I am going to give something, not receive something. The more I focused on what I am receiving—the perception of the audience, the interest of the audience, their perspective of me, their thoughts and feelings about my message—the more anxious I felt. The more I focused on what I am giving—an offering, an opportunity to serve, a chance to bring healing and hope, an invitation to love others—the less anxious I felt. Instantly. It was not about me at all. I am there to serve, not to perform. I am there to give, not to receive.

That little thought has shifted everything for me, and I can tell you with sincerity that even with a speaking engagement coming up in a few weeks in front of 8,000 people, my anxiety is low. Of course there will be the normal, physical jitters from adrenaline right before I get up there to speak, but my feelings are more anticipation and excitement rather than anxiety and fear. I am there to offer a gift. And however the audience chooses to receive that gift is on them, not me.

I know I've talked about my experience with public speaking, but I really believe that this one thought will change so much when it comes to our social anxiety in situations big and small. When you walk into a room, what is your focus? What is your fear? Do you find yourself worrying how you will be perceived and received, or is your focus on what you are there to give? Are you there to perform, or are you there to serve? Are you there to be liked, or to encourage and affirm others? Are you more fixated on what you have to give, or what you hope to receive? In that business meeting, are you able to see your attendance at the meeting and your feedback as a way of serving the company and the people around you? Are you able to shift your perspective, even when going through a drive-through to grab a coffee, that your social interaction is something that can bless and encourage the barista? When you step into a setting with new people, is your focus on how they are perceiving you or on how you can bless and encourage them?

We can't even begin to be good at social interactions when we're so fixated on the internal dialogue that centers around ourself and what we will receive or how we will be perceived. We can't even begin to get out of our head and step into giving to others when we're more perceptive of the signals coming toward us (what others think and feel about us) than the signals we're sending (the thoughts and feelings we get to convey toward others).

I don't know who you are, where you come from, or what you've been through, but I do know this: You have something to offer the world around you. You do. Your mere presence is a gift to this world and to the people around you. You have the ability as well as the responsibility to edify and encourage those around you (1 Thessalonians 5:11). You were created uniquely you, and the gift you have to offer the world is one-of-a-kind. There is no one who has anything like it, because there is only one version of you. So whether you're speaking to a crowd or meeting someone for the very first time, remember that you are there to give the gift of yourself. That is all you have to offer and all you have to give, and it is more than enough. It is only up to you to be the giver of that good gift. How it's received is out of your hands, out of your control, and outside the scope of your responsibility. So bring the good gifts that God has given you to give to your next social interaction and remember that it is better to give than to receive. And then watch how that one thought changes everything.

YOU HAVE SOMETHING TO OFFER THE WORLD AROUND YOU.

TAKE OWNERSHIP

1. On a scale of zero to ten (zero being no social anxiety, and ten being extreme social anxiety), what number do rate your social anxiety?

2. In a social setting, are you generally more focused on what you will receive and how you will be perceived or what you are going to give?

3. What are some underlying thoughts that fuel your social anxiety? Write them out and look for any themes. (For example: I wonder what they will think of me. Will they like me? Do I look okay in this outfit? Do I have anything to offer? Am I boring? Will they agree with what I'm saying?)

4. Reflect on this quote from the chapter: *You are going to give, not to receive* (page 175). How does that mindset shift change your perspective on social interactions? How might

it impact your next social interaction? What might you say, do, or how might you act differently if you held onto that shift in perspective?

If you struggle with moderate to severe levels of social anxiety that are extreme, persistent, and debilitating in your everyday life and interactions, and that are inhibiting your social and occupational goals, consider getting an accurate assessment from a mental health professional and seeking the help of mental health treatment by way of therapy and/or medication to help you take the next steps toward healing.

24

DEALING WITH DIFFICULT PEOPLE

Love from a Distance

If I ask you to think of the most difficult person in your life, who comes to mind?

I have a clear picture of who that is for me. This particular person was an acquaintance of mine until our interactions started to get rocky. It seemed like everything I said got turned around, misinterpreted, and twisted to make me look like I was saying something I wasn't. And the more I tried to interact, explain myself, or clarify the misunderstanding, the more it added fuel to the fire. I tried confronting this relational dynamic head on, but even that got turned around and misinterpreted. It got to a point where I realized that the best way to interact with this person was from a distance. Minimal interaction meant minimal room for misinterpretation and misrepresentation.

We're called to love all people. But there are some people who make it difficult to love them up close.

I think it's important to clarify that every single relationship has moments of difficulty. Even the healthiest relationships come with times of misunderstanding, misrepresentation, and misinterpretation. Even the safest people can speak out of line, say something hurtful, have an exaggerated emotional response, or get triggered by an interaction (see chapter 17 for more on emotional triggers). But when it comes to difficult relationships, it's important to understand there are levels of difficulty.

WE'RE CALLED TO LOVE ALL PEOPLE. BUT THERE ARE SOME PEOPLE WHO MAKE IT DIFFICULT TO LOVE THEM UP CLOSE.

A *healthy relationship* will have moments of difficulty. There will be arguments, disagreements, and misunderstandings. In a healthy relationship, the ultimate goal is reconciliation and reconnection. Both people in the relationship desire that, and though it may take a little time to get on the same page, eventually both parties take ownership, apologize, and move forward together. If we had to rate a healthy relationship on a scale of zero to ten (ten being the unhealthiest), we'd say it's in the zero-to-three range.

A *challenging relationship* is one in which there are more moments of conflict, tension, and arguments than in a healthy relationship. The goal of a challenging relationship is also to seek reconciliation and reconnection, but it may take a little more time, energy, and back-and-forth communication to get there. Both parties recognize that they have unhealthy traits that tend to come up in times of conflict, or moments of blame, but they work on trying to do things differently, taking ownership where they can, and moving toward healthy rather than defaulting to their unhealthy patterns. If we had to rate a challenging relationship on a scale of zero to ten (ten being the unhealthiest), we'd say it's in the four-to-five range.

A *difficult relationship* is one where there are more moments of conflict, tension, and arguments than there are moments of peace, joy, and connection. In this type of relationship, there tends to be more blame than ownership, and one (or both) parties often feel like they are misunderstood, misrepresented, or misinterpreted. The goal of one or both persons is to be heard, rather than to listen, and so communication tends to be very difficult and ends up being either one-sided or completely ineffective all together. Unhealthy cycles seem to come up more often than not. These are the type of relationships where we need to consider the role of loving at a distance and loving with limits. If we had to rate a difficult relationship on a scale of zero to ten (ten being the unhealthiest), we'd say it's in the six-to-eight range.

A *toxic relationship* is the next level of an unhealthy relationship. In this type of relationship, there are consistent and persistent patterns of dysfunction, high levels of misunderstanding, misinterpretation, misrepresentation, and even manipulation. If a difficult relationship has more challenging moments than connecting moments, a toxic relationship rarely sees the connecting moments and is primarily defined by the dysfunctional moments. One or both persons in the relationship refuse to take ownership, to apologize, or to try to see the other person's perspective. Communication ends up opening the door to name-calling, invalidating, blaming, and justifying unhealthy and hurtful behaviors. There's no such thing as ownership in a toxic relationship, only blame. In these types of relationships, the distance must increase to a very high level. If we had to rate a toxic relationship on a scale of zero to ten (ten being the unhealthiest), we'd say it's in the nine-to-ten range.

The last type of interaction I want to touch on goes beyond toxic and moves past what I would even refer to as a relationship and into the category of an *abusive interaction*. In this type of interaction, there are consistent patterns of deceit; betrayal; physical, sexual, or emotional aggression; or patterns of unaddressed addictions and/ or substance abuse. Once you've crossed into this territory, it's no longer about trying to keep the relationship because you can't call it a relationship when there is no "relating." Many times a toxic relationship bleeds over into an abusive relationship. In this type of interaction, you have to consider moving from high boundaries and limits to no contact. (If you find yourself in this type of relationship, or even wonder if you are, I urge you to meet with a professional counselor to process how to set limits and stay safe in this type of interaction.) If we had to rate this type of interaction on a scale of zero to ten (ten being the unhealthiest), we'd say it's in the eleven-plus range.

LOVE AND LIMITS

Here's why this matters: Your level of closeness should be equivalent to the level of the health of your relationship. The level of access and interaction you allow someone to have in your life should match the level of safety and responsibility in the relationship. We're called to love all people, but we're not called to love all people up close. There are some people who, because of their own lack of ownership, lack of health, and lack of insight and awareness, are people we have to learn to love at a distance. The unhealthier a relationship, the more distance we need to put in place as a protective barrier. Here's what this means practically.

1. Remember That You Can't Change People

The first step is realizing what we can and can't do. We can communicate our feelings, needs, and requests. But we can't change people. We can share what things we would like to see changed, but it's up to the person to change. Learning to love with limits means there's a level of *emotionally unhooking* from the difficult interaction.

We have to separate our emotions from the other person's reactions. We don't have to be up when they are up and down when they are down. We have to determine how we will choose to think, feel, and act in the situation despite their actions or lack thereof. Like I've said before, the only part of the recipe of the relationship we can change is the ingredients we bring to the table. Always go back to what you can and can't take ownership of.

2. Use "I" Statements

One of the number one things we teach in counseling about dealing with difficult people and difficult relationships is to focus on "I" statements rather than "you" statements. "You" statements put the focus on the other person, whereas "I" statements put the focus on your needs, feelings, and desires. A "you" statement, for example says, "You are so invalidating!" An "I" statement would word it by saying, "I feel very invalidated when we're having a difficult conversation." Focus on what you feel and what you need, rather than putting the focus on what the person needs to change.

3. Focus on the Behavior Patterns Rather Than the Person

Don't get caught in the trap of making it about the person, rather than about the pattern. When you start making it about the person and personalize it, you give the difficult person a reason to get defensive and tune you out instantly. So rather than saying, "You're a liar" (which personalizes the issue), focus on the pattern instead: "We seem to consistently have different perspectives on what happened. How can we get on the same page?" Instead of saying, "You're so defensive," try saying, "I notice that my feedback doesn't get communicated the way I intend. How can we work on this?" I think the concept of looking for patterns is really important because it helps us focus on what we want to see changed and make more significant progress. Sometimes we get caught up in looking at the *pain points*, which I define as isolated incidents of difficult behavior, instead of *patterns*, which are repeated cycles of difficult behavior. Identify and then address the pattern that you want to see changed in the relationship.

4. Be Clear with Your Boundaries

Boundaries are one of my favorite skill sets to teach. And even healthy relationships have boundaries. In fact, I would argue that one of the things that keeps relationships healthy *is* boundaries. But one thing I've found is that most people get boundaries totally wrong because they think a boundary is telling someone what you want them to do differently. For example, some people think a boundary is saying something like, "You need to stop calling me at 2:00 a.m. while I'm sleeping!" But that's not actually setting a boundary; that's giving a command. And those are very different things. Telling someone what to do is not a boundary, but telling them how you will respond to what they do is exactly what a boundary should be. So, in the example above, a boundary would be saying, "If you call me in the middle of the night, I won't pick up because it's not healthy for me to discuss something at that hour." A boundary is about *your* response more than it is about their behavior.

5. Follow Through with Your Boundaries

It's one step in the right direction to set a boundary, but the only thing that makes a difference is following through with your boundaries. If you tell someone you "won't pick up the phone" if they call you at 2:00 a.m., and then you answer their call, you haven't followed through with your boundary. If anything, you've reinforced the unhealthy behavior you're trying to eliminate from the relationship. You can't guarantee whether or not someone will respond to your boundary, so the only person who can keep the boundary is you, which means that you have the responsibility to keep the limits you set.

6. Love from a Distance

The healthier a relationship, the closer the proximity, and the higher levels of access you will give someone to your life. But the opposite is also true: The unhealthier a relationship is, the more distance you need to establish, and the less access you will give in the relationship. Loving with limits means an increase of distance and a decrease of access. For me, loving people from a distance has looked like:

- Decreased Engagement: Choosing not to respond to every single interaction from someone I am loving at a distance (texts, emails, phone calls, etc.).
- Decreased Priority: Choosing to reserve my schedule for the people whom I am loving up close, and decrease the prioritization of those whom I'm loving at a distance.
- Decreased Interactions: Choosing to have less communication points such as fewer phone calls or text messages, and intentionally spending less time together.
- Decreased Investment: Choosing to decrease what I give to the relationship, as well as decreasing my expectations of what I will receive from the relationship.
- Decreased Availability: Choosing not to feel obligated to say "yes" to invitations or opportunities to engage in the relationship.
- Decreased Trust: Choosing not to share valuable information or emotionally vulnerable conversations as a way of limiting access to my heart.

These are just some ideas to get you thinking of how you can set boundaries and learn to love difficult people at a distance. The unhealthier the relationship, the higher the boundaries and limits that need to be set. The Bible reminds us in Matthew 7:6 not to "throw your pearls before pigs" (ESV), which means don't give something valuable to those who will devalue it. Your heart is valuable, and it's worth protecting. "Above all else, guard your heart, for everything you do flows from it" (Proverbs 4:23). So guard your heart because it's yours to protect. Learn to love from a distance.

TAKE OWNERSHIP

1. Who are the most difficult people in your life currently? Out of the levels of health mentioned above, what level would you categorize your relationships with these people (healthy, challenging, difficult, toxic, or abusive)?

2. Is your level of access and availability equivalent to the level of health and safety in the relationships you have in my life? In which relationship does your access and availability need to increase or decrease?

3. When it comes to loving at a distance, which area do you struggle with the most? (Review the six categories on page 187, while keeping this in mind: *You can't change people.*)

4. What is one way I can begin to love from a distance and learn to set healthy limits and boundaries in my relationships with difficult people?

25

THE FEEDBACK LOOP

Is it Red, Yellow, or Green?

I've gotten some hate mail over the years.

Does that seem surprising for someone as kind, caring, and compassionate as I am? I thought so too, but it's true. There have been numerous occasions where I've received critical comments, infuriated emails, or degrading DMs, where someone was out to tell me what I did wrong, how much I offended them, or even what is wrong with me. It took me a little time to get used to this uninvited stream of negative feedback. I've been in this ministry space for a little over a decade, and I still remember the first time I got hateful comments on an article I wrote. I don't remember what the comments were, but I certainly remember how they made me feel: insecure and anxious. Since this type of public feedback was new to me back then, I didn't know how to deal with it. At the time, I put all feedback (whether it came from a random person online or from a good friend) on the same level, and in doing so, I allowed it to impact me more than it should have. Over the years, I've gotten much better at knowing how to handle these types of situations, but most importantly, I've learned that there are three different kinds of feedback, and each kind demands a completely different response.

Let me ask you this: When was the last time someone gave you some sort of feedback, whether in the form of a text or email, a face-to-face conversation, or a public comment? It might have been a mean or hateful comment, a constructive critique, a challenge or suggestion, or even an opinion about something you should do differently. Can you think of it? What was it about? How did it make you feel? Was it serious, or superficial? Now let me ask you this: What was your initial reaction to the feedback they gave you? How did you respond? What emotions did it bring up in you? How did you process the feedback given to you? To what level did you allow it to impact your life? Hold on to those feelings and reactions for a moment because we'll come back to them in a bit. And when we do, some of those feelings and reactions you had will be invited to stay, while others will be invited to go.

IS IT RED, GREEN, OR YELLOW?

I've come to realize that not all feedback is the same, and before we can even begin to accept feedback, we first have to learn to categorize it. The level at which we receive and process feedback should match the level of trust we have in the person giving it. To make it practical, I've started putting feedback into three categories: red, green, and yellow. Each category helps me process how seriously I should take the feedback and to what level I should allow it to impact my life.

Red: This is the easiest type of feedback to categorize because it typically comes from people I have no relationship with. For example, this could be an email from someone who read one of my books, a random comment on Instagram from someone I don't have a real-life relationship with, or an interaction with someone who doesn't know me well. The red category is for people who have *no* relationship with me, so when it comes to accepting feedback from them, red means *stop*. I will always stop before entertaining feedback from someone in the red zone because if the level of relationship should match the level to which I'm trusting and receiving the feedback, someone in the red zone has not earned my trust in any capacity. Therefore, their feedback can be set to the side and disregarded. The benefit of this is that when you aren't caught up in feedback that doesn't matter, you can focus in and concentrate on the feedback that actually does matter. You can imagine how much time and emotional energy this has freed up in my personal life, giving me the space and energy to focus on feedback that moves me toward development rather than discouragement.

Yellow: This category of feedback comes from people in one of two groups: 1. Those whom I have low-to-medium levels of relationship with and 2. Those who have high levels of credibility and safety (though not high levels of relationship). For example, people who have low-to-medium levels of relationship with me personally could be certain family members (cousins, aunts, uncles), friends (those outside of my core group), colleagues and coworkers, neighbors and those in my community, or people in my church family. An example of people with high levels of credibility and safety (though not high levels of relationship) could be a leader at my church, a reputable colleague in my field of work, or even someone in authority whom I have allowed myself to learn from (such as a boss, manager, or teacher). The yellow category could also include someone I am serving or leading, such as those who work for me or are in some capacity connected to me. The yellow category of feedback means that I receive it with some caution: I see it as an invitation toward personal growth and progress, but I don't assume it's 100 percent truth. I can take some, but I can also leave some of this feedback, because a low-to-medium relationship means a low-to-medium level of receiving feedback.

Green: This category of feedback comes from people whom I consider to be my core group, those with whom I am in high levels of relationship and who have earned high levels of trust. For me personally, there are only a few people I have chosen to put into this category, including my husband, my parents, my mentors, and a few of my best friends. These are the few people who have earned my trust and invested in our relationship deeply over the years. The green category of feedback is a level of feedback that I am willing to sit with, listen to, and pray about even if I don't always initially agree. It's a group of people whose words and feedback I have chosen to allow to have influence in shaping my life, and so I choose to see their feedback as an invitation for personal growth, healing, humility, and transformation in my life. That doesn't mean I will take *everything* they say as if it's God's truth because there are still times, even in the green zone, when feedback is listened to with respect and yet may not be fully or completely received. For me, this is when I would go to the One and Only Source, the One whom I go to with a heart that is 100 percent willing to receive the trustworthy feedback and conviction of the Holy Spirit. He is the One who helps us stay in alignment and gives us the wisdom and discernment to understand what we are invited to receive, even from the people we love and trust the most.

RECEIVING AND GIVING FEEDBACK

I think it's essential for us to be able to categorize the feedback we're given into these three levels because not only does it help us recognize the level to which we're invited to engage with the feedback, but it also helps us determine the level to which we should be giving feedback too.

I will never be able to comprehend or compute the mass amount of red zone feedback that people choose to post on social media, toward people they hardly know anything about, in comparison to the low level of real-life feedback given in our everyday green zone relationships. Take a moment and just read through the comments of any remotely controversial social media post (or save your time and energy and just take my word for it), and you'll see what I mean. There's never a shortage of the mass amount of judgmental, hurtful, rude, and wildly opinionated comments. We're so quick to allow our emotions of anger and offense and judgment to dictate the feedback we give to others, as a way of making *ourselves* feel better rather than seeking the goal of feedback: a gift of empowerment and encouragement to the people we love, an additional resource in their pursuit of becoming better, healthier, and stronger.

This is why Proverbs 27:6 is adamant: "Faithful are the wounds of a friend" (ESV). When feedback causes us discomfort or even pain, when it's from a faithful friend, it's a gift that can be received because it's ultimately for our good. This brings us back around to some of the initial feelings and reactions I asked you about at the start of this chapter, the ones I told you to hold on to for later: What is your initial reaction to the feedback that others give you? How do you respond? What emotions does feedback bring up in you? How did you process the feedback given to you? To what level did you allow it to impact your life? Do you interpret feedback as an offense, or do you see it as an opportunity?

As you go into the loop of giving and receiving feedback, start by categorizing the type of feedback it is, and then remember that proper feedback is an invitation for growth, healing, and transformation. So let's learn to give it and receive it with grace.

FEEDBACK IS AN INVITATION FOR GROWTH, HEALING, AND TRANSFORMATION.

TAKE OWNERSHIP

1. How do you typically handle feedback from people in the red, yellow, and green zones?

2. Have you ever found yourself struggling with feedback from someone in the red zone? Why do you think you allowed it to influence and impact you to that level?

3. List some people who are currently in your green zone when it comes to giving and receiving feedback.

4. Are you quick to see the giving and receiving of feedback as a *gift* and an *invitation*? Why or why not? Why might you tend to see feedback as an *offense* rather than an *opportunity*?

26

THE BEST-KEPT SOCIAL SECRET

Attachment Styles

I counseled a young woman who, after almost a year of dating, had yet to meet her boyfriend's family and friends. Not only that, but she also hadn't even had one phone call or interaction with them. Their dating life consisted only of interactions with one another. He was adamant that he wanted to take things slowly and that she would meet them when the timing was right. But the timing never seemed to be right, and she felt like he was always keeping her at a distance both emotionally and relationally, until they finally broke up. Fast forward a few months as she and I were processing the breakup. She was introduced to the concept of attachment styles for the very first time, and then it all began to make sense.

What if I told you there was a formula to the way you connected with people? What if I told you that the way you connected to others had less to do with your wiring, and more to do with the world you grew up in, the way you were raised, and the way you interacted in your childhood? But what if I told you that this formula could be altered, changed, and transformed and that you could learn to have the type of connections you desire just by changing the formula?

In counseling and psychology, we refer to this formula of how people connect as *attachment styles*. If you've done any amount of work with me or someone from my team, attended one of my online seminars, or read a previous book I've written, at some point you were introduced to the concept of attachment styles. It's such an important concept to understand that it comes up eventually with each client I work with.

Attachment styles are essentially the way that we learn to connect (or disconnect) to our feelings, as well as the way that we learn to connect (or disconnect) to others. The two go hand in hand because how we connect to our feelings has such an impact on how we connect to others. The more connected we are to our feelings and emotions, the more connected we will be to others. The less connected we are to our feelings and emotions, the less connected we will be to others. The reason for this is because emotions are connecting points. They are opportunities for us to connect with God, with ourselves, and with others. And so, attachment theory focuses on exactly *how* we connect. It groups attachment styles into two main categories: secure attachment and insecure attachment.

THE MORE CONNECTED WE ARE TO OUR FEELINGS AND EMOTIONS, THE MORE CONNECTED WE WILL BE TO OTHERS. THE LESS CONNECTED WE ARE TO OUR FEELINGS AND EMOTIONS, THE LESS CONNECTED WE WILL BE TO OTHERS.

Secure attachment refers to a healthy connection with my own emotions, as well as a healthy connection with others. It involves feelings of safety and security within myself and within my relationships. *Insecure* attachment, on the other hand, refers to an unhealthy attachment to my own emotions, as well as an unhealthy connection with others. It involves feelings of insecurity and a lack of safety within both myself and within my relationships.

In an insecure attachment, we struggle with how we feel about ourselves, as well as how we perceive others feel about us. And no matter how secure we are in our attachment style, deep down, we all struggle with aspects of insecure attachment. It's part of our human nature. And understanding our attachment style is one of the most important ways we put our people skills in context. Not only that, but understanding our attachment style can also help us connect more intentionally with the people in our lives.

Let's dig a little deeper into the three categories of *insecure* attachment styles.

ANXIOUS ATTACHMENT

People with an anxious attachment style often feel insecure and deeply aware of their relationships with others. They worry about whether or not people will stay, like them, and remain loyal to them. In order to keep people close, people with anxious attachment have a tendency to go above and beyond in their relationships, doing more than their fair share in order to be loved and accepted. They fear that if they don't do enough, the relationship will dissolve. Because of this, they have a tendency to find themselves in one-sided relationships where they are doing most of the giving and getting very little in return. In some cases, they can come across as clingy or needy because they are desperately seeking connection with others. They also tend to share their emotions freely, which can make others, specifically those who are not used to this level of emotional expression, uncomfortable.

People with an anxious attachment style may have come from a background where they had to fix broken relationships, or mend a chaotic family situation. It was their role to make sure people stayed, it was their job to cultivate intimacy, and maybe it was even their responsibility to take care of the emotional needs of those around them. They were often put in the role of giving, rather than in the role of receiving. Because of this, they tend to put the role of maintaining close relationships on their own shoulders, taking on full responsibility. They carry a false belief that if they stop working, fixing, trying, forgiving, giving, helping, or connecting, the relationship will fail. They end up doing far more than their fair share, and in turn, struggling with feelings of bitterness, resentment, and emotional exhaustion.

AVOIDANT ATTACHMENT

People in the avoidant attachment style have learned to have a level of separation from their emotions, as well as a level of separation from close relationships. They falsely believe that feelings push people away, rather than bring people close. Not only are they uncomfortable or out of touch with their own feelings, but they are also uncomfortable with too much closeness in a relationship and prefer to rely on themselves as much as possible. They feel more in control when they don't have to rely on others to meet their needs. Because of this, they tend to keep people, as well as their own emotions, at a distance. In other words, avoidant attachment style learns to shut down or avoid certain experiences as a way of self-protection.

People with avoidant attachment style may come from a past where emotions were not allowed to be seen or felt, or where emotions were seen as a weakness rather than a strength. Maybe they grew up in a family where it was better to be logical than emotional, so they ignored their feelings and used their head instead. Or maybe they grew up in an environment where their emotional needs were never met, so they learned to repress their needs rather than live with unmet needs. Maybe they responded by learning to take care of themselves and therefore decreasing their need for others. Whatever the reason, when they live in a shut-down way, they become more comfortable with keeping people at a distance rather than bringing them close.

SHAME-BASED ATTACHMENT

Those with a shame-based attachment style tend to blame themselves for their relationship failures. They might critique, shame, and blame themselves as motivation to try to become better. They may even feel as though they're not good enough for relationships, or that they don't deserve relationships. Their relationship with their emotions is inconsistent because they have strong feelings, but they don't trust their feelings nor themselves in general. People with a shame-based attachment are more likely to trust what others think, feel, and believe than to trust their own intuition. They spend their life trying to prove to themselves and to others that they are worth loving. Though they have a deep desire for relationships, they tend to push others away out of fear that people will end up rejecting them or hurting them.

People who struggle with this type of attachment may come from a childhood where there was abuse or violence. Because shame was put on them at a young age, they continue to carry that mindset of shame into their adulthood. Maybe they come from a background where there was inconsistency with how they were loved: one day they were praised, the next day they were mistreated, so they assume that they are treated based on what they deserve. They tend to interpret people's negative behaviors toward them to mean there must be something wrong with them or that they're doing something wrong, so they put a lot of pressure on themselves. They find themselves wishing they could be good enough, smart enough, or adequate enough. Shame-based attachment style keeps people at a distance, because ultimately, they don't believe they are good enough for intimate relationships and have a fear of being exposed for who they really are.

Now that we've talked through the different attachment styles, I want you to take a moment to reflect on your relationship with others, with yourself, and with God. I want you to tune in to your tendency to either pull away or desperately try to draw near in fear that others will pull away. We were created for relationships by a God who made us to be in relationship with Him. But sometimes our own insecurities, fears, and trauma keep us from attaching the way we were meant to attach. Because how you connect (or disconnect) with people has so much to do with the way you attached to your caregivers and those in other significant relationships in your formative years. The roles that we played in childhood often become the roles we play out in adulthood unless we choose to interrupt the pattern.

WE WERE CREATED FOR RELATIONSHIPS BY A GOD WHO MADE US TO BE IN RELATIONSHIP WITH HIM.

Understanding our attachment styles helps us understand the motivation, the *why*, behind the way we connect or disconnect from others. If you're learning about attachment styles for the first time in this chapter, there's probably a lot to process right now. If this is a familiar concept to you, it's a good time to reassess and recalibrate your attachment to the significant people in your life and identify which relationships might still need healing.

Understanding your attachment style is the secret to creating healthy relationships because we get to see our connections with others objectively, through the context of this important formula of social development. So whether we're talking about our relationship with ourselves and our feelings, significant others in our lives, or our relationship with God, having a healthy understanding of our attachment styles and taking the time to both honor and heal from the roles we played in childhood will help us move from insecure relationships to a place of secure, stable, and strong relationships—with ourselves, with others, and with God.

TAKE OWNERSHIP

1. Which of the three insecure attachment styles do you identify with the most? (It's possible to identify with more than one.)

2. What past situations, traumatic experiences, or formative relationships may have had a role in creating that attachment style?

3. How does that specific attachment style play out in your everyday relationships? When and with whom do you see it the most?

4. What is one relationship in which you would like to move toward a secure attachment? Is there one or more experiences from your past that may need to be addressed or

healed from to move toward secure attachments in your present? Take a moment in prayer and ask God to spotlight any experiences that may need deeper healing.[1]

For deeper learning on attachment styles, as well as a list of other important topics, check out our list of recommended resources at https://debrafileta.com/dfcnresources/.

27

EMOTIONAL INTELLIGENCE

People Smarts

If you were stranded on a deserted island and had the choice to be stranded with someone who possessed a very high IQ (intelligence quotient) but low EQ (emotional quotient), or someone with a very high EQ but low IQ, which person would you choose? If you're anything like me, I would 100 percent choose the person with a high IQ because I would be desperately hoping that their high level of intellect and intelligence could find a way to get us off that island ASAP, MacGyver style! (Did I just date myself?)

Now, let me change the question a little bit and ask you this: If you had to choose one of those same two people to interact with on a daily basis, to do life with, and to have any type of meaningful relationship with, which one of them would you choose? That changes my answer quite a bit, because when it comes to everyday living and being and relating and interacting, I would always, always, always choose the person with a high EQ, because EQ changes everything. I would even go so far as to say that in my personal and professional opinion, EQ is the number one thing that impacts our people skills.

Most of us understand the concept of IQ (a measurement of personal intelligence), but very few people are even aware of the concept of EQ (a measurement of our emotional intelligence). So let's start by defining the concept of emotional quotient (which I will also refer to as emotional intelligence): Emotional intelligence is the ability to understand, manage, and express your emotions, as well as having an awareness of the emotions of those around you. People with a high level of emotional intelligence can identify what they feel, understand where those feelings might be coming from, and make connections to how those feelings may affect their behavior. People with a high level of emotional intelligence are also acutely aware of what others might be feeling around them and are in tune to the emotional expressions that are being communicated (both verbally and nonverbally) from the people they are with. To put it simply, emotional intelligence comes down to four things: emotional awareness, emotional expression, emotional control, and emotional interpretation.

One of my favorite things about Jesus, as evidenced through Scripture, is how emotionally intelligent He was. I think that's one of the reasons He was so effective at dealing with and interacting with all kinds of people. He was so in tune to what He was feeling, so intentional about expressing His feelings, yet so deliberate in managing His feelings (John 15:10-11; Luke 19:41; John 11:35; John 4:6; Matthew 23:33; Matthew 9:36; Luke 22:44). I spend a lot of time unpacking the constructs of emotional intelligence and the emotional health of Jesus in my book *Are You Really OK?* But for now, let's look at the four basic components to emotional intelligence.

EMOTIONAL AWARENESS

It might sound simple to be aware of your emotions, but this can be so difficult for people who have grown up suppressing, repressing, minimizing, or ignoring their emotions. I met a man who told me that he "doesn't really have many emotions." But it's not that he doesn't have many emotions, because we are all made in the image of God with a broad spectrum of emotions; it's that he's not in tune to his emotions. You see, sometimes our feelings get put on mute either because they make us feel weak or because they feel so powerful or so overwhelming that we don't think we can handle them. And so we turn down the dial or press the mute button on our emotional control system, without even realizing that we're blocking them out. This was the case for this gentleman as well. As we unpacked his story, I discovered that he had been through severe childhood trauma. Without his awareness, his emotions had essentially been "turned down" during that season of life for him to survive it. And he had lived with his emotional mute button on ever since.

If emotions (especially difficult ones) are uncomfortable for you, it makes sense that you desire to flee from uncomfortable things. The problem is, we often confuse *uncomfortable* for *harmful*. But just because something is uncomfortable doesn't mean it's harmful. In fact, sometimes the most uncomfortable things are the very things that grow and strengthen us. I often equate emotional awareness and emotional intelligence to going to the gym for physical fitness. It's an exercise that we get to practice for the strengthening of our muscles. There are times when it will be uncomfortable, but in those moments, we are getting stronger and increasing our capacity to feel and experience life.

The level to which we allow ourselves to feel the difficult feelings is also the level to which we'll experience the glorious ones as well. What you feel deeply on one side, you'll feel deeply on the other side too.

THE LEVEL TO WHICH WE ALLOW OURSELVES TO FEEL THE DIFFICULT FEELINGS IS ALSO THE LEVEL TO WHICH WE'LL EXPERIENCE THE GLORIOUS ONES AS WELL.

EMOTIONAL EXPRESSION

If emotional awareness is your ability to be in tune to your feelings, emotional expression is your ability to communicate and convey those feelings to the people around you. It's one thing to feel something; it's another thing altogether to communicate that feeling in an effective way. Many of the lessons we addressed previously, including body language, tone of voice, levels of communication, and vulnerability, are the very things that help you to convey the emotions you are experiencing to the people around you. It takes intentionality to take what's going on inside of you and share it with the people around you.

It's important not to assume that people will know how you feel or that they will be able to perceive what you might be feeling and experiencing simply by how you are behaving. Without even realizing it, sometimes our external behavior is actually incongruent to what's going on inside of us. We might be acting one way yet feeling something completely different. Earlier we talked about how emotions are connecting points (to God, self, and others), and emotional expression allows us to clearly communicate what's going on inside of us and to intentionally connect with the people around us.

EMOTIONAL CONTROL

Just because you feel something doesn't make it true. Once, my college roommates and I pulled into our driveway to see someone walking around inside our house through the dimly lit windows. The level of fear and panic that filled all of us in that moment is a feeling I won't soon forget, as one of my roommates frantically picked up her phone to dial 9-1-1 while I backed out of that driveway like I was some sort of NASCAR driver. We were filled with feelings of fear and anxiety because our brain's alarm system went off (thanks, amygdala), signaling the release of chemicals that kicked our sympathetic nervous response (the fight-or-flight reaction) into full gear. A few seconds later, and right before I sped off, our 90-year-old landlord opened the front door and informed us, "Not to worry, girls; it's just me." Apparently, she couldn't find her favorite pan and thought that maybe she had left it in one of the storage closets in the house we were renting from her. No one was home, she said, so she just "let herself in." Oh, Mary. Turns out, our feelings weren't exactly accurate.

The power of emotional response is that it alerts our body to the fact that something needs to be paid attention to. I've explained how our emotions are the SOS system God placed inside of us to signal us to pay attention. But just because we feel something doesn't make it true. Our emotions are *real*, but they don't always reflect *reality*. The emotions of fear and anxiety we felt at the thought of an intruder were *real* emotions. But they didn't reflect *reality* in the fact that it was actually our 90-year-old landlord playing a game of hide-and-go-seek with her frying pan. Our emotions aren't meant to know everything; they're simply meant to respond. This is why the concept of emotional control or emotional management is very important to our level of emotional intelligence. We have to be so aware and in tune to what we are feeling, but then we have to learn to align those feelings with the truth. If not kept in check with reality, feelings can wreak havoc in our lives. Emotions are meant to signal us, but they are not meant to lead us.

EMOTIONAL INTERPRETATION

Have you ever been in a situation where you could just *feel* the emotions exuding from someone? One time a group of us were invited over to our friends' house for a dinner party, and they had just had an argument right before we all got there (we didn't know that at the time). The tension between them was so thick you could cut it with a knife. The edgy remarks, cool body language, and icy tone between them was just as awkward as you can imagine. A little while into the evening, they started warming up to one another again, and as the tension began to melt they eventually told us that they had had a pretty big fight before we arrived, which is why they were acting so emotionally distant. "Oh really?" said another friend of ours. "I actually didn't even notice!" At first I thought he was just being sarcastic, but he was dead serious. He was so engrossed in the food, drinks, and entertainment that he literally didn't notice the emotional environment. I think it's easier for people who are internally aware (those with a tendency toward introspection and insight) to observe the internal emotions of others, than for those who are more externally aware (those with a tendency toward observing their external environment like food and drinks!).

EMOTIONS ARE MEANT TO SIGNAL US, BUT THEY ARE NOT MEANT TO LEAD US.

My husband and I are actually very different in this way. I'm much more internally aware and he's much more externally aware. We can be driving down the road together in the car, and while I'm thinking about what I'm feeling and what he might be feeling and what I'm feeling about what he's feeling, he's thinking about how awesome it is that our car just hit 55,555 miles on the dot, noticing that the neighbors just got their driveway repaved, observing the fact that the license plate number of the car in front of us is made up of only vowels (and probably crunching the probability of that happening in his head), all while wondering why Google Maps is telling him to go left when he knows that going right is the much faster option. For people who are externally aware, it takes more effort to stop processing the external world and be intentional about tuning into someone's internal world (and even their own internal world!).

We can't manage the feelings of others, and we can't change the feelings of others, but we can certainly pay attention to the feelings of others. While I'm *not* talking about simply making assumptions about how someone might be feeling, which can be off-putting if you're wrong, I *am* talking about the concept of reading the room. It's the concept of being aware and in tune to the emotional cues, the verbals and nonverbals someone is communicating, and then adjusting your behavior and response accordingly.

WHAT'S YOUR EQ?

While there's no completely objective and accurate measurement of emotional intelligence, here are a few statements to consider as you work on raising your emotional IQ and increasing your people smarts:

- I am good at identifying the emotions I am feeling.
- I am often aware when my emotions shift and change.
- I can easily identify what the people around me are feeling.
- I am usually in control over my feelings and my reactions to my feelings.
- I don't allow my feelings to get in the way of what I need to do socially, occupationally, or relationally.
- I can easily read the body language of others.
- I intentionally observe how people might be feeling and what they might be experiencing.
- I do a good job expressing my internal feelings to the people around me.
- I consider myself an internally aware person.

- I am good at managing my feelings and calming myself when I am stressed or anxious.
- When I feel something, I can quickly trace where that feeling came from and why I am experiencing that feeling.
- I can gauge what people around me might be feeling based on their actions and reactions.
- I talk about my feelings on a regular basis.
- I have a wide range of emotions, and I can identify many more emotions than the basics of happy, sad, mad, and glad.
- I am comfortable hearing about what other people are feeling and experiencing.
- I don't often lose my temper, because I know what's going on beneath the anger and can express those feelings in other ways.

These are just a few statements to get you thinking. The more you're able to check off and affirm, the closer you are to increasing your EQ. And the better your EQ, the better your people skills.

TAKE OWNERSHIP

1. Do you tend to be more internally aware or externally aware? What are some signs of this in your day-to-day life and interactions?

2. How in tune are you to your internal emotional world throughout the day on a scale of zero to ten (zero being not aware, and ten being always aware)?

3. What are some ways you practice emotional expression with the people in your everyday life? If you can't think of any, what's one way you can begin?

4. How many statements were you able to check off regarding your emotional intelligence? What is one area you need to work on?

28

TECHNOFERENCE

From Screen Up to Screen Down

We were on the way to a restaurant recently when my husband, John, observed how many people around us were on their phones simultaneously while driving down the highway. Now, I understand we live in a world of self-driving cars, but we're not talking Teslas here. There was definitely no self-drive mode happening in these automobiles. Since we were on the theme of screen obsession, once we got to the restaurant, I couldn't help but notice how many people were on their phones, screens glued to their faces, all while "socializing" with the people they were there with.

But is it surprising? It's so commonplace these days that you hardly even notice when it's happening all around you. Take a few minutes to people-watch practically anywhere, and it won't take long to see how tech-obsessed our culture has become. From walking around talking into Instagram stories, to Googling the latest NFL scores, to watching movies and videos on YouTube, to scrolling through endless pictures and limitless comments, there's never a shortage of something that needs to be checked, watched, shared, liked, or posted. There's never a shortage of reasons why I should pick up my phone at this moment. Even as I'm typing this sentence, I'm fighting off the urge to check my phone to see what time the package I ordered is coming so I can stay focused on this chapter about tech issues. It's undeniable how the rise of technology has had an impact on our people skills and, more so, our lack thereof.

So much so, that the term *technoference* was coined in 2012, describing the phenomenon of the interference and interruptions technology has on our social relationships. One study defined technoference as "the intrusion of technology into personal relationships."[1] In this digital age, when we're faced with our screens from the moment we wake up to the moment our heads hit the pillow at night, there's no doubt in my mind that technology is one of the most significant intrusions to our social connections and relationships.

Just take a look at some of these facts and you'll see what I mean.

- The average American picks up his or her phone 204 times a day.[2] That comes out to approximately every five minutes around the clock.
- The average American gets seven hours and three minutes of screen time a day.[3]
- A typical teenager spends one hour and 27 minutes on social media[4] and one hour and 46 minutes gaming.[5]
- Seventy percent of couples experience conflict related to screen time.[6]
- Higher rates of technoference lead to worse relationship quality, increased conflict, a more negative mood, and less positive face-to-face interactions.[7]
- Increased screen time leads to feelings of decreased social connectedness.[8]

- Technoference has become so commonplace that the term *phubbing* has been used to describe the act of being snubbed by someone who is more interested in their technology than their real-life relationships.[9]

Technology is clearly getting in the way of our relationships. We've gotten to a point where we've exchanged the intimacy of real-life relationships for the inanimate. Our marriages, families, children, and friends are coming in second place to our screens. The question is: What do we do about it?

WE'VE EXCHANGED THE INTIMACY OF REAL-LIFE RELATIONSHIPS FOR THE INANIMATE.

SCREEN UP TO SCREEN DOWN

I don't think the answer to our technoference issues is to get rid of our devices altogether (though for people with addiction issues, this may be something you need to do for a certain amount of time). But I do think the most important thing we can do is to set protective boundaries around technology so that we can be intentional about connecting with the people in our lives. Here's what I suggest.

Limit Your Screen Time

Before you can limit your screen time, you have to be aware of your screen time. You should have an idea of the average daily time you spend on your screen. This is easy information to find out by checking your screen time usage on your phone. Now add to that the amount of time you spend watching TV, or gaming on a device or computer. Anyone in the four-to-six-hour range per day (outside of direct work hours) needs to be on high alert with their boundaries, because their relationships are starting to see the negative effects of their screen time. And for those in the six-plus-hours-per-day category, I can predict significant struggles already exist in their relationships. Because increased screen time equals decreased relationship quality. There's no other way around it. No matter how many excuses you try to make for yourself.

In addition to the negative effects screens have on our relationships, increased screen time is also associated with lower self-esteem, an increase in mental health struggles and addiction issues, slower learning and memory decline, as well as cognitive decline.[10] Be intentional about setting boundaries with how much you use your phone and devices by taking advantage of things like app limits, turning off notifications so you're not constantly drawn to your phone, and using the do-not-disturb feature throughout the day. Consider taking regular fasts from social media or from using your screens altogether for a few hours, a few days, and even up to a longer period of time such as a screen-free week or a social-media-free month to reset your need to stay connected to your screen and increase your desire to connect with the people around you. Sometimes you don't realize how connected you are to your devices until you set limits around them.

Tech-Free Spaces

It's important to have tech-free spaces and zones in your life, and even more so for those of us who have kids because an unhealthy relationship with screens leads to unhealthy relationships with the people around us. Sometimes it helps to have tangible times when you enter a tech-free zone and tangible places to put your devices each day. Some people like to use some sort of a box to put their phones in, so they're actually out of sight. In our family we'll often use a particular desk in the house to put all our devices on during dinner so no one is tempted to reach into their pocket to check something real quick or pick up a phone call. It gives us an opportunity to have intentional time to talk and not be distracted. Think through what tech free spaces might look like in your life and for your family, and then begin to practice those boundaries.

Don't Give in to the Urge

The worst thing you can do for your bad habits is to give in to them. Especially when you're trying to decrease your screen use, don't give in to the urge to check, post, Google, comment, or do something else really quickly no matter how practical or significant it may feel. If it's that important, write it down on a piece of paper and set aside a time where you can check what you need to check and do what you need to do later. The funny thing is, most of those things end up passing on and not being that important in the long run. Things can wait. But the people who really matter to you shouldn't have to.

The more you give in to the urge, the more you're allowing your brain to get caught in the dopamine loop (the body's reward system), which will reinforce the very cycle you're trying to break. But the more you can fight the urge to check or pick up that device, the faster you'll be able to break free from its grip. Be intentional about fighting the urge.

Practice Being Present

Being here and now is a gift. In fact, this moment, right here and right now, is the only moment that's guaranteed in your life. When I was writing my book *Soul Care*, studying the healthy rhythms that Jesus practiced, I couldn't help but stand in awe at His ability to be present and to savor the moment He was in with the people He was with. He knew how to be right here and right now even during some of the most difficult times in His life where it would have been so tempting to escape physically, emotionally, or mentally to another location (Matthew 26:20). It would have been easy to distract Himself from what was going on. Yet He remained present. Sometimes what we're doing when we pick up a screen is we're trying to escape mentally and emotionally from something. Setting boundaries with our devices can give us the space to dig a little deeper and really process what it is we're trying to distract ourselves from.

THIS MOMENT, RIGHT HERE AND RIGHT NOW, IS THE ONLY MOMENT THAT'S GUARANTEED IN YOUR LIFE.

Learning to be present with the people around us means we're intentional about staying in the moment with them: seeing them, hearing them, staying with them. And not only with the people around us, but also with the beauty that's all around us (God's incredible creation), as well as the complexity of what's going on inside of us (our internal emotions, thoughts, motivations and reactions). We can't be present and distracted at the same time. We can't savor life while we're on our screens. The two are mutually exclusive.

How often do you find yourself phubbing the people around you because your phone becomes more interesting than your fellowship? Even if that's not what we really believe deep down, that's the exact message we're sending to the people around us. Not only that, but we're missing so much of life by looking down at our devices rather than looking around as life is happening all around us. You weren't meant to see life through a screen, you were meant to take it in with all your senses. The more you're screening, the less you're living. So be intentional with putting your screens down and decreasing the technoference in your life. And watch what it does for your relationships.

TAKE OWNERSHIP

1. What would you guess is your average daily screen time?

   What is your guess of how many times you pick up your phone each day?

   What is your guess of how much time you spend on social media each day?

   Now, go and check the actual data, and compare it with what you guessed (this data can be found under your screen time settings). Was it more or less than what you expected?

2. If you are in the four-to-six-hour range: In what ways have you seen your screen time start to impact your relationships? What boundaries do you need to establish and follow through on to decrease your screen time and increase the quality of your relationships?

3. If you are in the six-plus-hour range: What might you be using screen time to escape from emotionally, mentally, or physically in your life? How can you begin dealing with some of those underlying issues so that you can begin to set healthier boundaries with your devices?

4. Take some time to write out a *technoference plan* of ways you will set boundaries and limits around your device so that you can focus on increasing the quality of your relationships. Write out at least three practical things you will do starting this week.

29

FIND CONNECTING POINTS

Get in the Zone

Anyone who knows my husband knows he's the king of bargaining. For him, there's no shame in the game. He's been known to bargain anywhere—from farmers markets to big brand stores like Walmart, Best Buy, and Costco. I guess it's the Middle Eastern in him. The deals he's been able to get from simply investing in a few extra minutes of conversation and clearly and directly asking for what he wants are too many to count and always leave me wide-eyed. Like the time we walked out of a department store with a $35 brand-new bike for our daughter's fourth birthday. He was a broke medical student, and I was still in graduate school, so we could barely afford groceries, much less the bike our little girl wanted. But with a few minutes of conversation and a little negotiating, he convinced the manager to sell him the display model of the bike at 90 percent off and get it off his hands. God's grace, paired with a little personal directness, goes a long way. If you ever meet John and want to get him talking, just ask him about some of the bargains he's made and watch his eyes light up.

Most of the reason people fail to strike a deal when it comes to bargaining, negotiating, or even communicating in general is because they fail to try to find the middle ground. What this comes down to is a skill set: the skill of learning to give and take to find what works for both parties. Expert negotiators call this the ZOPA: the zone of possible agreement. It's the middle zone where both parties in a conversation find a landing point, a place where they can agree and compromise and connect. The zone in which both parties get something out of it. The zone where they have common ground, common goals, and an overlap in interest. The ZOPA is an incredibly important concept in business, but it's really important in relationships too. If you can't find the ZOPA between two people, you'll fail in trying to connect. You'll fail in moving forward. You'll fail in building relationships.

WHAT DO WE HAVE IN COMMON?

My good friend Sarah is one of the most extroverted, socially connected people I know. We became friends in college, and ever since I've known her, I've always been fascinated by how gifted she is at social interactions. It amazes me to see how many people she knows and loves, and how many people know and love her. She becomes fast friends with people who seem to have absolutely nothing in common with her.

Take, for instance, a few weeks ago when she joined me at a conference where I was speaking. She was running my book table during my book signing and meet and greet, and I kid you not, she found something in common with each person who approached that table! She made so many friends that weekend. I couldn't believe some of the conversations I was hearing coming from that side of the room, of places, people, and things she had in common with people she had just met for the first time! So much so, that I would find myself leaning in and listening just because the conversations were so intriguing!

And as I've watched her interact over the years, I've realized that one thing she's really good at is finding the ZOPA: the overlap in common ground between her and the person she's talking to. She could be talking to someone with a completely different religious belief system, political affiliation, personality type, and ethical and moral standard than her own, and she can still find the overlap. She will always find the connecting point.

I think of it like a Venn diagram between two different people. You both have differences, but you also have something in common. Because no matter how different two people might be, if you're really looking for it, you'll always find an overlap. Even if the overlap is as basic as the fact that you are both two human beings. There's still a lot in common there! I mean, you technically have 99.9 percent of the same genes (don't believe me, look it up). Watching Sarah interact over the years has made me realize the importance of finding common ground, a connecting point, no matter who it is I might be interacting with. We're called to connect. We're called to find the middle ground because that is where we can grow in our interactions, our connections, and our relationships with the people God brings into our lives. Learning how to find the ZOPA is something that you can apply to so many different relationships from your marriage, to your children, to your friends, to your neighbors, to your colleagues and coworkers and everyone in between.

NO MATTER HOW DIFFERENT TWO PEOPLE MIGHT BE, IF YOU'RE REALLY LOOKING FOR IT, YOU'LL ALWAYS FIND AN OVERLAP.

One thing I love about Jesus is how good He was at connecting with people who were completely, absolutely, utterly different from Him. So much so, that He got criticized for hanging out with people whom others didn't think He should have anything in common with at all (Matthew 9:10-13; Mark 2:15-22; Luke 5:29-39; John 4:27). He was interacting with sinners—no, He was dining with them—sitting around a table breaking bread with them and finding common ground. Eating a meal with someone during Jesus's time didn't just mean sharing food with them; it meant identifying with them. I wish I could have been a fly on the wall of those many interactions, just to hear Jesus get in the zone with people who were so unlike Him. He found ways to connect with them like no one else could.

GET IN THE ZONE

If someone were to watch all your interactions throughout any given week, what would they say about your ability to find the ZOPA? What about with people who are different from you? People who hold different political views? Different morals and values? Different perspectives? Different personalities? We're so quick to tell people what we don't agree with or why their perspective is wrong, or to try to get people to hear our perspective and our opinions. Just look at any online thread about anything remotely disagreeable and the comments will always prove to be more divisive than connecting. So what's your tendency to get in the zone?

I can already sense a few of you resisting this concept, because you want to tell me that we shouldn't agree with people who don't believe in the same things we believe. And I agree with you (see how I found the ZOPA there?). I'm not talking about agreeing about everything. And I'm definitely not talking about compromising our personal morals and values. But I am talking about the concept of finding places to agree: connecting points where relationships can begin to take root. When people feel seen, heard, and noticed, they let their walls down.

WHEN PEOPLE FEEL SEEN, HEARD, AND NOTICED, THEY LET THEIR WALLS DOWN.

If we really want to own our impact and make the most of every interaction, we've got to learn how to connect in meaningful ways, to get in the zone with the people in our lives. This could look like:

• • •

In an argument with your spouse, you change your goal from correcting to connecting and try to find a place of agreement rather than trying to be right and make your case.

• • •

When engaging with someone for the first time, you seek to learn something about them and find a topic you have in common to connect in conversation.

• • •

In the car ride home with your kids, you listen to their experiences and emotions and connect with them on the similar things you felt and experienced when you were their age.

• • •

If there's tension at work, you are intentional with your coworkers to find a common ground on your goals, ideas, or vision for the future.

• • •

When interacting with someone you typically disagree with, you change your perspective to try to find a place of commonality and see it as an opportunity to listen and connect.

• • •

Be intentional in assessing your ability to get in the zone and stay in the zone with the interactions you have this week. Keep the concept of the ZOPA (the zone of possible agreement) in your mind and watch how a simple business strategy can begin to change your relationships and help you make the most of your interactions.

TAKE OWNERSHIP

1. Do you tend to notice the differences during your interactions with people or the similarities? If you had to rate yourself on a scale of zero to ten (zero being never able to find common ground, and ten being always able to find common ground), what number would you rate yourself?

2. Think about the person you seem to disagree with the most or get along with the least. Fill out this Venn diagram with regard to your differences, and then take some time to think through the things you may have in common.

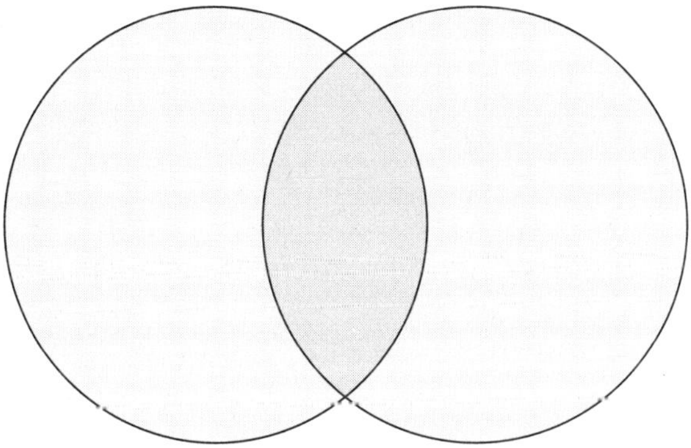

3. Write down five questions you can ask if your goal is to find the middle ground when you're interacting with someone.

4. Consider one difficult relationship in which God may be inviting you to take the next step in finding connecting points and getting in the ZOPA. Take some time to pray and ask God to lead and guide you.

30

COMPARISON VERSUS CONNECTION

They Aren't Your Measuring Stick

I'm pretty open about the fact that I hate running. I'm not a runner, never have been, never will be. I love walking, and I'm even content to fast-walk, but try to get me to pick up the pace just a little more, and I will completely lose my joy. In fact, I often say that if you ever catch me running, you should probably start running too because it likely means something big, mean, and scary is chasing after us.

Even though I'm not a runner myself, I'm genuinely amazed at the amount of discipline, strength, and commitment it takes to master this sport and the life lessons we can learn from it. I watch the Olympics with awe, as the runners discipline their bodies in preparation for this once-in-a-lifetime, breathtaking sprint to the finish line. There's a well-known story about a historic 1954 race, known as the Miracle Mile, between two of the fastest men in the world at that time, Roger Bannister and John Landy. Both men had been the first in history to ever break a four-minute mile (Bannister broke the record first, followed by Landy just a month later, who beat Bannister's record by 1.4 seconds). And now, they were up against each other in this momentous race at the British Empire Games, as the entire world watched in awe.

As they got to the last lap, Landy was ahead and expected to win, but in his uncertainty, he glanced over his left shoulder to see where Bannister was in comparison to him. And as he did, he slowed his stride by a fraction of a second, which allowed Bannister to take the lead and ultimately break through the tape in first place, winning the race by less than a fraction of a second.[1] "I would have won the race if I hadn't looked back," Landy expressed after the race in regret. Just one tiny glance, one fraction of a second, one moment of distraction, cost him everything.

One thing I know to be true about the sport of running is that, no matter what, you never look away from the finish line. As tempting as it might be to stop and look around, to see where others are in comparison to you, you have to fight the urge to look to your right or to your left and just stay focused. Looking anywhere but straight ahead will always slow you down, physically and mentally, and may sabotage your entire race.

DON'T LOOK AROUND

This happens in running, but it's also true to life. We're each called to run our own race and keep our eyes on the finish line. "Let us throw off everything that hinders and the sin that so easily entangles. And let us run with perseverance the race marked out for us, fixing our eyes on Jesus, the pioneer and perfecter of faith" (Hebrews 12:1-2). We're asked to stay focused, get rid of everything that distracts us, and fix our eyes on Jesus.

But it's easier said than done. We live in a world that literally sets us up for comparison. Just pick up your phone for two seconds, and look at any social media app, and you'll be bombarded with a sneak peek of what everyone else is doing. We can get instant access to see how they look today, what they're wearing, who they're dating, what they ate for breakfast, where they are on vacation, how much money they're earning per month, how their house is decorated, how successful their job is, what grades their kids are getting, how their marriage is thriving (or at least that's what the picture shows), and any other story they choose to share for us to see. We're tempted by comparison within seconds of opening our apps. We can scroll and scroll through an entire gallery of people to compare ourselves to. They become our measuring stick: the standard by which we measure our own value, worth, beauty, accomplishments, body image, and success. And the funny thing is, we willingly do this to ourselves and allow our FOMO (fear of missing out) to rage and our insecurity to rise. If we're not actively fighting against comparison, we'll always succumb to the temptation of looking around. But others are not our measuring stick. They are not the standard. They can have no say until we allow them to have a say.

IF WE'RE NOT ACTIVELY FIGHTING AGAINST COMPARISON, WE'LL ALWAYS SUCCUMB TO THE TEMPTATION OF LOOKING AROUND.

And not only that, but when we do succumb to the temptation of allowing them to be the standard, we always come out feeling miserable. I don't have to prove to you that studies show us that comparison leads to feelings of depression, anxiety, and insecurity because you know it to be true in your own life. You never feel better after falling short. And if you're *winning* for even a moment, you know it's just a matter of time until you're *failing* again when people are the measuring stick of your value and worth because there will always be someone who's ahead. It's a fast track to misery.

This is why the Bible is so clear that we shouldn't look over and compare, because it only leads to distraction (Galatians 6:4-5). But even Jesus's own disciples struggled with this tendency to look around, rather than looking straight ahead and fixing their eyes on Him. John 21 paints a scene of Jesus, having an intimate conversation with His friend and follower, Peter. He's giving him a personal pep talk, strengthening him, and preparing him for what's ahead on his journey, and then intimately says to him, "Peter, follow me" (verse 19). He's essentially saying: *Peter, I need you to stay focused. I need you to stay close.*

What does Peter do next? He makes the same mistake that John Landy would make 2,000 years later: he turns and looks back (John 21:20). He looks at the disciple walking behind them and starts to compare his life to another's. "What about him?" (John 21:21). "What is that to you?" Jesus says back (John 21:22).

What does his story have to do with your story? What does her story have to do with your story? What does their life have to do with your life? Stay focused. Don't get distracted. They are not your measuring stick. Stay focused on what God has set before you and don't look to the right or to the left because it will only slow you down and hold you back. *I need you to stay focused. I need you to stay close.*

YOU CAN'T CONNECT WHEN YOU COMPARE

I think the trickiest thing about this whole concept of comparison isn't even the fact that comparison makes us feel miserable and distracts us from our journey, but that it also prevents us from connecting with others. You can't connect with the people you're comparing yourself to because it can never be a genuine connection when the goal is competition. When the goal is "I want to be better than you,"

I can't genuinely wish you well, encourage you along your journey, and give you what you need to succeed. I can't love you if I'm trying to get ahead of you. Sometimes the very thing that keeps us from connecting well with the people whom God has put into our lives is the dark and dangerous streak of comparison. It can be so subtle that we stop noticing it in our own lives, but let me assure you, the people around us can feel it. And it taints the relationship.

YOU CAN'T CONNECT WITH THE PEOPLE YOU'RE COMPARING YOURSELF TO BECAUSE IT CAN NEVER BE A GENUINE CONNECTION WHEN THE GOAL IS COMPETITION.

But when the goal becomes my own journey, at my own pace, in my own way, following what God has called me to do, I can readily give you what you need for your own journey. Because now it's not a competition; it's a collaboration. When we each have our own personal race to run, and the goal is simply to get to the end of our own designated race, it becomes a team effort to make sure everyone we know gets to their own finish line. Because you can't connect when you're competing, but you can thrive in connecting when you're collaborating.

FOLLOW ME

I don't know how tempting it is for you to look around, to the right or to the left, and see where others are along their journey. And I don't know what your personal race looks like right now, or what goals, dreams, and accomplishments you hope to attain. I don't know if you're struggling in comparing your appearance, your relationship status, your finances, your personal hardships, or your family dynamics with those of others. But I do know this: *They* are not your measuring stick. And the only One who has the authority to hold the measuring stick is the One who calls you worthy, the One who calls you friend, the One who calls you child, and the One who calls you to stay close. *Don't get distracted. Stay focused. Fix your eyes on Me.*

"Follow me," Jesus says (John 21:19). In a culture where following others is the norm, and the term we use for the people we choose to compare our lives to on social media, the platform that tends to be the biggest trap for our comparison, I find it to be a very relevant invitation for today. Who are *you* following?

TAKE OWNERSHIP

1. When it comes to comparing your life with others, where do you find yourself tempted the most? (For example: social media, with a certain group of friends, or around colleagues and coworkers.)

2. What is the area you find yourself struggling with the most when it comes to comparison? (For example: appearance, finances, career, family, relationships, hardships, or success.)

3. What mindset shifts do you need to make to see your journey as your own rather than comparing your journey to others?

4. "You can't connect when you compare." What are your thoughts on that concept? Do you think comparison has tainted your relationships? If so, which area of your life might you need to confess and repent of comparison, and begin seeking a mindset of collaboration instead?

31

TO LOVE AND TO LIKE

Your Highest Calling

Google *T-shirts for introverts* and a wide variety (of surprisingly larger proportions than I expected) will come up. Here were some of the ones that made me laugh out loud with their lingo:

- Introverted: But willing to talk to plants.
- You read my T-shirt. That's enough social interaction for one day.
- 3 Ways to Engage an Introvert: 1. Don't 2. Don't 3. Seriously, Don't.
- Introverts Unite: Separately, in our own homes!
- I'm an Introvert. (Please don't talk to me.)
- No small talk, please.
- It's too "peopley" outside.

- I wanna be where the people aren't.
- Do Not Disturb: ON.

Okay, you can tell I got a kick out of them because they just about all made me laugh. Especially when I consider the introverts in my life. (And it's probably just a coincidence, but the people who really like plants in my life are all introverts!) As a counselor, I find it fascinating to see the difference between introverts, those who prefer alone time to recharge and fill up, and extroverts, those who prefer being with people to recharge and fill up.

But I think there are a lot of misconceptions regarding what an introvert or an extrovert is, and one of the biggest misconceptions is that extroverts like people, while introverts don't. But that rhetoric is completely unfair and untrue. It's not that introverts don't like people; it's that being around people takes up more emotional, mental, and even physical energy for them than it does for extroverts. If you consider yourself an introvert because you don't like people, then you are most likely just using that as an excuse to mask your dysfunction. Liking people is not an introvert or extrovert thing; it's a *Christian* thing. It's a *Jesus* thing. And it's all too common these days to hear someone casually say, "I don't really like people," or "I'm allergic to people." If we're honest, we've gotten a little too comfortable with the self-protection, the isolation, the withdrawal, and the social distance. And it's there, in our isolated bubbles, that the enemy is cornering us and taking us out one, by one, by one.

LIKING PEOPLE IS NOT AN INTROVERT OR EXTROVERT THING; IT'S A *CHRISTIAN* THING. IT'S A *JESUS* THING.

TO LOVE AND TO LIKE

When we look at God's Word, the call for Christians is clear: to love people. I mean, to really, really love people. So much so, that Jesus camped out on this same commandment over and over again in some of the final days of His time here on earth. "A new command I give you: Love one another. As I have loved you, so you must love one another" (John 13:34). Again and again, in Jesus's final words to His disciples, He reminded them that love is our highest calling: "Love each other as I have loved you. Greater love has no one than this: to lay down one's life for one's friends. You are my friends if you do what I command" (John 15:12-14). If He could only get one thing into our hearts and into our heads before He went to heaven, He wanted us to be known by one thing, and one thing alone: *love*. "By this everyone will know that you are my disciples, if you love one another" (John 13:35). But how can we love people if we don't even like them?

It doesn't matter if you consider yourself to be an introvert or an extrovert. The calling is clear: people are to be a priority. Next to loving God, you are to love and honor people the way that you love and honor yourself: "'Love the Lord your God with all your heart and with all your soul and with all your mind and with all your strength.' The second is this: 'Love your neighbor as yourself.' There is no commandment greater than these" (Mark 12:30-31). In fact, the Bible goes on to tell us that if you *don't* love people, then you have to seriously consider whether or not you love God. "If anyone says, 'I love God,' and hates his brother, he is a liar; for he who does not love his brother whom he has seen cannot love God whom he has not seen" (1 John 4:20 ESV).

Listen to me loud and clear when I say this: There's no exceptions here to personality type, trauma history, rejection wounds, or even a lack of people skills. No one is exempt from this command. You cannot opt out of this invitation. You are called to love people and to love them well. Because how can you say you love God, if you don't really love His children? As a mom of four kids, I can relate to this concept. My kids are my people. And one of the best ways you can show me that you love me is when you love my people. It means more to me when someone treats my kids well than when they treat me well. But it also hurts much more when the opposite happens. They are my flesh and blood, and I won't believe anything you say if you tell me you love me but then treat one of them with unkindness or disrespect.

I am so passionate about the subject of this book, *People Skills*, because I really believe that it can help us learn how to love people well. Most people I interact with have a desire to love people well; they just don't always get it right because they're lacking in the practical skill set of what it actually means to convey that love to the people in their lives. They might have love in their hearts, but the love doesn't make its way into the lives of others because it's being blocked, misunderstood, misinterpreted, or simply miscommunicated. As I said in the beginning of this book, it's not usually a lack of love that keeps us from connecting with the people around us; it's a lack of skill.

Throughout all the pages and chapters of this book that you've read (and will hopefully reread), I hope and pray you've sincerely and authentically taken the time to search your heart and ask yourself to be honest about the ways you are conveying the love of God through the way you interact with people, and consider how you are convoluting the love of God by your lack of people skills.

Maybe you've discovered that your listening skills could use some work, that your empathy levels aren't where they should be, or that your body language conveys something completely opposite of what's going on inside of you. Maybe you've realized your technology habits are getting in the way of your relationships, or that you're not as good at apologizing as you thought, or that you're caught in a trap of comparison that's keeping you stuck in your relationships. Maybe you've identified struggles with unforgiveness, pride, or insecurity that are holding you back from loving the way God has called you to love.

Whatever it is that God has brought to your attention as you've read through the chapters of this book, I encourage you to see it as an invitation—an invitation to own your impact, strengthen your relationships, and make every interaction count. An invitation to take inventory of how you come across and to adjust what is in your power and control in order to have the healthiest relationships possible with the many different people God has brought into your life, from the most significant interactions to the seemingly insignificant ones. Because from the perspective of the Father, how you treat His children matters. People matter to Him. And because they matter to Him, they should matter to us.

PEOPLE MATTER TO HIM. AND BECAUSE THEY MATTER TO HIM, THEY SHOULD MATTER TO US.

May God help us take seriously this high calling, and may we learn to really see people and love people well. Because sometimes, the only thing that's inhibiting our love is a lack of skill. Let's learn to increase our people skills and watch how that transforms our relationships, our marriage, our families, our ministries, and in turn, our entire lives. Here's to a new season of learning to love better and do relationships well. Because our relationships will only be as strong as our skills.

TAKE OWNERSHIP

1. Do you consider yourself an introvert or an extrovert? Why? How does being an introvert or extrovert affect your relationships and interactions?

2. Do you tend to withdraw, self-protect, isolate, or distance yourself in relationships? When do you see this happening most often, and why?

3. Consider the social circles in your current life: family, close friends, community, career, etc. How have you been intentional to convey God's love in each of these different social circles? What is something you can do practically to be intentional to show love in each of these social groups?

4. Take a look at the table of contents. Which people skill from the chapters of this book is the main one you need to work on or strengthen in your life in the immediate future? What are some steps you will take to put this into action this coming week? Now, take a moment to list the top three people skills you would like to focus on in the coming months.

NOTES

CHAPTER 1: PEOPLE SKILLS

1. I co-authored a book with Gary Thomas called *Married Sex: A Christian Couple's Guide to Reimagining Your Love Life* (Zondervan, 2021).
2. Study Finds, "The Lonely Crowd: 40% of Adults Go Days Without Face-to-Face Interaction," April 1, 2024, https://studyfinds.org/lonely-adults-without-interaction/.

CHAPTER 3: FIRST IMPRESSIONS

1. Debra Fileta, *Reset: Powerful Habits to Own Your Thoughts, Understand Your Feelings, and Change Your Life* (Harvest House, 2023).

CHAPTER 4: CONVERSATION SKILLS

1. Martin B. Copenhaver, *Jesus Is the Question: The 307 Questions Jesus Asked and the 3 He Answered* (Abingdon Press, 2014).

CHAPTER 6: TELL THAT TO YOUR FACE

1. Jeff Thompson, "Is Nonverbal Communication a Numbers Games?," Psychology Today, September 30, 2011, https://www.psychologytoday.com/us/blog/beyond-words/201109/is-nonverbal-communication-a-numbers-game.
2. Carol Kinsey Goman, "5 Ways Body Language Impacts Leadership Results," Forbes, August 26, 2018, https://www.forbes.com/sites/carolkinseygoman/2018/08/26/5-ways-body-language-impacts-leadership-results/.

CHAPTER 7: POSITIVE AFFIRMATION

1. Russell A. Barkley, *Your Defiant Child: Eight Steps to Better Behavior* (The Guildford Press, 2013).

CHAPTER 9: WHAT'S YOUR TYPE?

1. For a much deeper dive on understanding your *why* and becoming aware of your needs, check out my book *Soul Care: *Find Life-Giving Rhythms *Live Restored *Avoid Burnout *Discover Unspeakable Joy* (Harvest House, 2024).

2. For additional support in dealing with your past, check out my incredible team of faith-forward counselors at DebraFileta.com/counseling.

CHAPTER 10: LISTENING SKILLS

1. Nelson Dellis, *Remember It!: The Names of People You Meet, All of Your Passwords, Where You Left Your Keys, and Everything Else You Tend to Forget* (Abrams Image, 2018).
2. Learn more about the Speaker Listener Technique in my book *Choosing Marriage: Why It Has to Start with We >Me* (Harvest House, 2018), 70-74.

CHAPTER 11: BE REAL

1. For a deeper dive on the topic of self-discovery and self-awareness, check out my book *Reset.*

CHAPTER 13: DEALING WITH REJECTION

1. For more on identifying and dealing with triggers, check out my book *Reset.*

CHAPTER 14: THE ART OF AN APOLOGY

1. Jeremy C. Anderson, Wolfgang Linden, Martine E. Habra, "Influence of Apologies and Trait Hostility on Recovery from Anger," *Journal of Behavioral Medicine* 29, no. 4 (2006): 347-58, doi: 10.1007/s10865-006-9062-7.

CHAPTER 16: YOUR SOCIAL TEMPERATURE

1. Dan Charles, "Study Links Warm Hands, Warm Heart," NPR, October 23, 2008, https://www.npr.org/2008/10/23/96041598/study-links-warm-hands-warm-heart. This is the original study: L.E. Williams and J.A. Bargh, "Experiencing Physical Warmth Promotes Interpersonal Warmth," *Science* 322, (2008): 606-607, https://psycnet.apa.org/record/2008-16045-002.
2. Sing Lau, "The Effect of Smiling on Person Perception," *The Journal of Social Psychology* 117, no. 1 (2010): 63-67, doi: 10.1080/00224545.1982.9713408.
3. Michael W. Kraus, "Voice-Only Communication Enhances Empathic Accuracy," Yale University, School of Management, https://static1.squarespace.com/static/5432c0d8e4b0fc3eccdb0500/t/58a3af349f74565ea7d27f32/1487122231232/voice-only-communication-enhances-empathic-accuracy.pdf.

CHAPTER 18: PEOPLE PLEASING

1. Talk To Me: With Candace Cameron Bure & Talk To Me: With Jinger Duggar, Debra Fileta, host, *Talk To Me: The Debra Fileta Podcast*, podcast, season 10, episode 320, "People Pleasers — Candace Cameron Bure," October 29, 2024, https://truelovedates.com/people-pleasers-candace-cameron-bure/ and season 10, episode 353, "On -Air Counseling Session with Jinger Dugger Vuolo," June 17, 2025 https://truelovedates.com/on-air-counseling-session-with-jinger-dugger-vuolo/

CHAPTER 19: SET THE TONE

1. Caroline Catmure, Vincent Walsh, and Cecilia Heyes, "Associative Sequence Learning: The Role of Experience in the Development of Imitation and the Mirror System," *Philosophical Transactions of the Royal Society B*, August 27, 2009, doi: 10.1098/rstb.2009.0048.

2. Ke Ma, et al., "Mood Migration: How Enfacing a Smile Makes You Happier," *Cognition* 151 (2016): 52-62, doi: 10.1016/j.cognition.2016.02.018.
3. Laura Petitta, et al., "Cognitive Failures in Response to Emotional Contagion: Their Effects on Workplace Accidents," *Accident Analysis & Prevention* 125 (2019): 165-173, doi: 10.1016/j.aap.2019.01.018.
4. If emotional intelligence is the area you would like to grow in, check out my book *Are You Really OK?* for a deep dive into emotional awareness, emotional expression, and emotional control. *Are You Really OK?: Getting Real About Who You Are, How You're Doing, and Why It Matters* (Harvest House, 2021).

CHAPTER 20: PRACTICE HUMOR

1. Lester E. Hewitt, "Student Perceptions of Traits Desired in Themselves as Dating and Marriage Partners," *Marriage and Family Living* 20, no. 4 (1958): 344-349, doi: 10.2307/348256.
2. Rod A. Martin, et al., "Individual Differences in Uses of Humor and Their Relation to Psychological Well-Being: Development of the Humor Styles Questionnaire," *Journal of Research in Personality* 37, no. 1 (2003): 48-75, doi: 10.1016/S0092-6566(02)00534-2.
3. Claudia M. Haase, et al., "Short Alleles, Bigger Smiles? The Effect of 5-HTTLPR on Positive Emotional Expressions," *Emotion* 15, no. 4 (2015): 438-448, doi:10.1037/emo0000074.

CHAPTER 21: WE ALL HAVE A LITTLE NARCISSUS IN US

1. *Diagnostic and Statistical Manual of Mental Disorders*, 5th ed., Text Revision (American Psychiatric Association Publishing, 2022), 669-670.

CHAPTER 22: THE H WORD

1. Billy Hallowell, "'All Glory to God': Eagles Coach, QB Openly Praise the Lord After Super Bowl LIX Victory," CBN, February 10, 2025, https://cbn.com/news/entertainment/all-glory-god-eagles-coach-qb-openly-praise-lord-after-super-bowl-lix-victory.
2. Thomas A. Tarrants, "Pride and Humility," C.S. Lewis Institute, December 4, 2011, https://www.cslewisinstitute.org/resources/pride-and-humility/.

CHAPTER 23: SOCIAL ANXIETY

1. For some people, extreme, persistent, and debilitating social anxiety is indicative of an overactive nervous system response, whether due to trauma or other physiological and psychological factors and may require an official diagnosis (Social Anxiety Disorder) and treatment by way of mental health counseling and/or medication.

CHAPTER 26: THE BEST-KEPT SOCIAL SECRET

1. Consider working with someone from our team of faith-forward counselors to help you on your journey at DebraFileta.com/counseling.

CHAPTER 28: TECHNOFERENCE

1. M.S. Neeraj, "Connected or Disconnected? Exploring Technoference and Its Impact on Interpersonal Relationships Among Youth," *International Review of Psychiatry* 37, no. 1 (2024): 59-66, doi: 10.1080/09540261.2024.2442410.

2. Alan Friedman, "You Won't Believe the Number of Months the Average American Wasted Checking His Phone in 2024," Phone Arena, December 29, 2024, https://www.phonearena.com/news/survey-shows-how-much-americans-use-their-phones_id166216.

3. "Average Screen Time Statistics," Yellow Bus ABA, March 5, 2025, https://www.yellowbusaba.com/post/average-screen-time-statistics.

4. Fabio Duarte, "Alarming Average Screen Time Statistics (2025)," Exploding Topics, updated March 26, 2025, https://explodingtopics.com/blog/screen-time-stats.

5. Fabio Duarte, "Alarming Average Screen Time Statistics (2025)."

6. Sat Nam Therapy, "Screen Time: A Couples Therapist's Perspective on the Destructive Force in Relationships," Sam Nam Therapy, October 22, 2024, https://satnamtherapy.com/Posts/Screen-Time-A-Couples-Therapists-Perspective-on-the-Destructive-Force-in-Relationships.

7. Brandon T. McDaniel and Michelle Drouin, "Daily Technology Interruptions and Emotional and Relational Well-Being," *Computers in Human Behavior* 99 (2019): 1-8, doi: 10.1016/j.chb.2019.04.027.

8. Christine Anderl, Marlise K. Hofer, and Frances S. Chen, "Directly-Measured Smartphone Screen Time Predicts Well-Being and Feelings of Social Connectedness," *Journal of Social and Personal Relationships* 41, no. 5 (2023), doi: 10.1177/02654075231158300.

9. Varoth Chotpitayasunondh and Karen M. Douglas, "How 'Phubbing' Becomes the Norm: The Antecedents and Consequences of Snubbing Via Smartphone," *Computers in Human Behavior* 63 (2016): 9-18, doi: 10.1016/j.chb.2016.05.018.

10. Eliana Neophytou, Laurie, A. Manwell, and Roelof Eikelboom, "Effects of Excessive Screen Time on Neurodevelopment, Learning, Memory, Mental Health, and Neurodegeneration: A Scoping Review," *International Journal of Mental Health and Addiction* 19 (2021): 724-744, doi: 10.1007/s11469-019-00182-2.

CHAPTER 30: COMPARISON VERSUS CONNECTION

1. Frank Litsky and William McDonald, "John Landy Dies at 91; Dueled Roger Bannister in 'Mile of the Century,'" *The New York Times*, updated February 7, 2025, https://www.nytimes.com/2022/02/25/john-landy-dead.html.

ACKNOWLEDGMENTS

I'll never take lightly the high privilege and great responsibility that comes with publishing a book and releasing it into the world. And I'll never take lightly the people, behind the scenes, who help to turn this message into the reality of the book you hold in your hand. I'm so grateful to my team at Harvest House, specifically Audrey, Lindsay, Bob, Sherrie, and so many others who play a role in getting this book out into the world. I've said it before and I will say it again, it's a team that feels more like friends and family. And for that, I am so grateful.

I'll never take lightly the fact that you, the reader, chose to put this book into your hands. Thank you for trusting me with this message, and for allowing me access to your heart. The most incredible part about this platform that God has entrusted me with is getting to meet incredible people like you and walk alongside of you on the journey of becoming healthy and whole: mentally, emotionally, spiritually, physically, and relationally. It's one thing to read one of my books, but some of you have read all nine of them so far, and I consider that the highest compliment. So, from the bottom of my heart, thank you.

And I'll never take lightly the gift of my family, close friends, and the deep community that God has given me to sharpen, refine, and enhance my people skills. You can't learn what you don't practice, and I am grateful to those I get to love, and those who love me back—for allowing me to practice, learn, and grow in our relationships. I love my people. And I am so grateful to each and every one of you. May God help me to love you better and better, and to convey His love to each of you and not convolute it.